THE
BRAND
SYMPHONY

Orchestrate your marketing strategy
and scale your service business

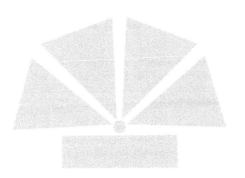

JILL PRINGLE

The Brand Symphony

First published in August 2019
Writing Matters Publishing (UK)
info@writingmatterspublishing.com
www.writingmatterspublishing.com

ISBN 978-1-912774-35-7 (e-book)
ISBN 978-1-912774-34-0 (pbk)

brandsymphonymarketing.com

Contents

Dedication

For Vivien Pike, who taught me to sing in tune with others

And my father, who made me practise.

Foreword

At *everywoman* we've spent the past two decades breaking down barriers for women in business and influencing the enterprise support provision for women in the UK. Our extensive experience and longstanding cross-industry relationships place us at the centre of the female business community. This has given us unique insight into the many challenges business owners face. When it comes to marketing, our research shows many have a respect for its ability to tip a business into another stratosphere, but many do not know how to do that.

As a business owner you are the conductor in the orchestra, the buck stops with you and everyone looks to you to steer the direction. Time and resource are often limited and as businesses and products scale it becomes even more important and challenging to be clear about what you offer, who your audience is, and all available routes to market.

A robust marketing strategy and a proposition that can be easily communicated are key to success. However, it can be difficult to execute this, especially as many business owners don't come with any kind of marketing experience.

That's why it's fantastic to see Jill, an *everywoman* *Ambassador*, sharing her extensive experience in marketing to champion fellow business owners and help them in this key area.

This book provides a simple framework and practical exercises to help you create a strategy, communicate your proposition and share your *brand symphony* with the right audiences.

Well done Jill, much applauded!

Karen Gill MBE

Co-founder *everywoman*

everywoman was founded by Maxine Benson MBE and Karen Gill MBE in 1999. With a presence in over 100 countries and a successful active network of over 20,000 members, it is a global digital network that drives the development of businesswomen at all levels, in all sectors including entrepreneurs.

At A Glance

Musical and performance metaphors are often paired with success especially business success. For example, customer service is often compared to dancing and choreography. In this book, the metaphor of an *orchestra* is paired to *branding.*

While *The Brand Symphony* was written for established smaller service industries, companies typically employing between 10-50 employees with revenues ranging £2-7M, it is in an invaluable marketing and branding reference for any sized company.

This book will walk you through the orchestrate method – 35 individual exercises for you and your marketer that will help you write, orchestrate and conduct your own *Brand Symphony.*

For more details or help using this methodology visit

brandsymphonymarketing.com

The concept that underpins *The Brand Symphony* can be seen in the diagram below:

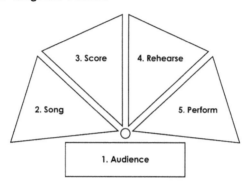

Each stage of this *Orchestrate Method* has seven steps:

	Audience	Song	Score	Rehearse	Perform
1	Consistency review	Benefits first	Start, stop, change, continue	Sing the song yourself	Sales funnel
2	Direct customer insight	Your business category	Products to value	Start, stop, continue again	Propsect process
3	Competitive set	What you do	Pricing model alignment	Customer journey map	Campaign plan
4	Name your ideal customer	Alternative solutions	Places you're seen	Defining moments	Elevator pitch
5	Who you serve (and don't)	The biggest benefit	Promotional messages	Targeting success	On-song checks
6	Audience insight summary	Write your value proposition	Physical evidence	Harmony & counterpoint	Tempo checks
7	Draw your customer	Stress test	People, values and behaviours	Dressrehearsal	Avoid shiny new toys

Overture

overture

/ˈəʊvətj(ʊ)ə/

noun

noun: overture; plural noun: overtures

1. an orchestral piece at the beginning of an opera, play, etc. the overture to Mozart's *Don Giovanni*

   synonyms: prelude, introduction, opening, introductory movement, voluntary; *rare* verset *the overture to Don Giovanni*

2. an introduction to something more substantial. *the talks were no more than an overture to a long debate*

   synonyms: preliminary, prelude, curtain-raiser, introduction, lead-in, precursor, forerunner, harbinger, herald, start, beginning; *informal* opener *the talks were no more than the overture to a long debate*

Becoming A Musical Marketer

I always used to say that I *fell* into marketing. At school I wanted to be a music teacher. Music was my best subject so it seemed the natural career path. I also knew no-one in my circle who was in business, so it never occurred to me that I could lead or contribute to one.

I went back to University to study a *Masters in Marketing* when I was 27. I had been working as Sales and Marketing Manager for a London orchestra for five years and was looking to progress and get my next job. No one outside of the classical music industry would employ me because what they saw on my CV was a music degree and no formal marketing training. The fact that I'd turned out to be quite a good marketer had no evidence other than my success in one role. And so, when I graduated with my *Marketing Masters,* I played my musical background down to get my next job. It went on the hobbies list.

It was only in an interview for my last permanent role as a CMO that I clocked what I said. I studied music before I studied marketing, and what music and marketing have in common is the need for both analytical and creative skills to be successful. After 20 plus years of a successful marketing career I had realised that my musical skills were actually a path to that success. And I'd been using them every day.

I grew up in Sheffield in the 1970s. I was lucky to be born there. Firstly, because I was born with severe hip dysplasia and the city happened to have a leading children's hospital that specialised in pediatric orthopedics. And secondly, because the socialist council heavily funded the arts, which meant that I also got the best musical training, for free. I don't really know why I first got into playing music - other than the fact that my parents both liked Rogers and Hammerstein musicals and fought over who was best - Frank Sinatra or Tony Bennett. I guess it was also because it was something I could *join*. Due to the hip dysplasia pretty much all team sports were out. So my team sports were recorder club, guitar club, brass band and eventually choir. It was a way of getting the spotlight that wasn't limited by being *differently*-abled.

At junior school my music teacher encouraged me to sing. I'm not sure I was actually that good but knowing myself, I suspect I was very enthusiastic! Then one day, when I was 11, the head of peripatetic singing for South Yorkshire came to our school. Vivien Pike ran a city choir and was looking for new members. Most of the girls in the choir came from the more affluent side of the city - where singing lessons were funded by the schools that employed her. But the council wanted a representation of people from less privileged backgrounds. I almost didn't audition because the choir clashed with Girl Guides, but my music teacher pushed hard. Ironically, I was on a Guides camping trip in Devon when I heard I'd got in.

One year later, the choir won the first ever BBC televised *Choir of the Year* competition in the UK. It was my first experience of winning as a team. And of getting things right, piece by piece, to build a performance.

Vivien was big on discipline. Almost 20 years later we

did a reunion concert with Lesley Garrett (who Vivien also taught to sing) and when Vivien walked on stage to take the rehearsal, everyone immediately stopped talking and sat up straight. We all laughed about it later but it was ingrained. She had trained us in the first role of being a musician. To listen. To her and to each other.

She also taught every girl in the choir individually - so she knew our personal as well as our collective capabilities. She was able to blend us perfectly - we won competitions because everyone was in the right part and knew where we were supposed to fit. She made us move parts as our voices changed through puberty and we were happy to try what she recommended because it worked.

We also knew what she expected. There was a very clear value proposition behind this girls' choir and through her we all knew and felt it. That value proposition was about *excellence.*

It was also about commitment - we all had to play our own part. Once the note-bashing was done we had to learn and practice the music individually, in our separate parts and as a whole. We had to teach ourselves as well as expect to be taught. This was not a *go on the one day training course and you're done* approach.

Over the next few years, whenever we travelled to competitions or festivals, people in other youth choirs had heard of us though they'd never met us or heard us sing. We weren't just a choir, we were a *brand.*

I think it was in his Stanford Address that Steve Jobs said; '*... you can only join the dots looking backwards.'* Now in my late 40s, I can see that I have copied much of what I learned from Vivien in my approach to building marketing teams and brands. A great logo or a great product don't make a brand (although they do help); *people make a brand work.* People deciding to contribute to a common goal and be part of something bigger than themselves.

I cut my teeth building marketing teams in a *yellow pages*-type company. I remember a new CEO asking me how I had developed such a good team. My new internet marketing team was hand-picked to work together and I'd thought about that as I built it. They weren't all the same type of people but they did buy into a collective goal and shared values around doing good work. They also had a very aggressive sales culture to work in - which in musical terms provided counterpoint (more on this later). In all the organisations in which I've built and led marketing teams I've approached their brand as a musical performance.

A performance that first a marketing team, and then all the employees in an organisation can contribute to day in, day out.

Fast forward another 15 years and I'm now a marketing strategy consultant and mentor for *service businesses.* What I bring is not just the marketing strategy (*what* to do and *how* to do it) but also an approach to *orchestrating* that across an organisation.

Or to put it another way. I take their tune and help them orchestrate, rehearse and perform it like a Beethoven Symphony.

At school I wanted to be a music teacher. It turns out that I am. I teach the music of marketing.

SECTION 1

BRAND AS PERFORMANCE

Chapter One

THE MUSIC OF MARKETING

One of the reasons I decided to write this book was because of the similar challenges I saw Managing Directors and Marketers face, just from opposite sides of the table. Both were frustrated with each other and the way that marketing was working - or not - in their organisation. What they each wanted to achieve they couldn't find a way to implement, together.

This book is about getting MDs and their marketers on the same page about what marketing is there to do for your organisation. And helping you to create the right environment for marketing to succeed.

This first chapter is the Prelude. It will take you through the key themes of this book and help you understand if this approach is right for you. Specifically, I will outline what marketing is and why it's about more than getting clicks. I will discuss what role marketing needs to play in your organisation as you grow, and why scaling a business is hard - because the mindset of the leader needs to change from that of composer to conductor.

My experience has taught me that thinking more like a musician can help you and your team build a standout brand. Orchestration is the key to successful marketing, especially in a service business, and in this chapter I'll outline the five steps to getting that right.

In many organisations, marketing is seen as sales support. Graduates leaving university with a marketing degree are quickly disillusioned that the models they learned are not used or welcomed. They make the mistake of trying to be a strategist without a broader commercial understanding of the business, so they can't make it relevant (or their attempt isn't taken seriously). On the other side of the table, the MD doesn't want to spend days working through models, even if they would help the marketer frame what they're trying to do.

One of the first things I ask marketing teams when I join a new organisation is *what activity they're doing.* And then I take each activity and ask *why they do it; what's its purpose?* The results are usually illuminating because ninety percent of the time, the answer really is *we don't know.* They might say to get leads but they can't explain *how* that piece of collateral is used and whether it is indeed turning into business. The more honest answers are soon *'Because Jim the sales director told us to do it* or even *It was all I could get signed off.'*

It would be very easy to believe that this is happening because the marketer isn't any good. In a few cases it might be that their calling is elsewhere but often the problem is that the organisation isn't hearing what the marketer is trying to say. Perhaps because they're not using your language.

Imagine if you came into work and just sent things out that other people had written for you, designed for you and told you who to send them to and how.

It's very easy for marketing to become the *admin overspill* department. The things your PA or the receptionist doesn't have time to do. Organise the Christmas party. Organise a sales meeting. In some cases your marketing person might even be your last PA who wanted to get a career in marketing but has no formal training.

In small organisations we all multi-task and muck in. It's part of the fun. But as we see later in this book, it's your job to give the marketer the right role in the performance.

Some of today's marketing trends don't help you to do this. Digital Marketing has become a discipline because technology enables so much *communication*. I have put that word in italics for a reason - because communication is about connection and social media doesn't always help the right people absorb your message.

I'm always grateful when someone on the marketing team grew up in the social age and is therefore intuitive of how to execute it well. But the rise of Digital Marketing has led to an obsession with clicks. And marketing has lapped it up - because for years it's been seen as *unmeasurable* and suddenly we can count what people are doing.

Marketing automation platforms can link people's journeys from social media into the sales funnel.

Whilst that can be helpful, it has bred a lack of emphasis on things like targeting and positioning the message. Which are the essence of marketing strategy. Delivering *clicks* and *likes* does not require your marketer to understand the commercial drivers of your business or what you want to be famous for. Marketing strategy does. And some of those models your marketer learned at university will help them, but they will need you to engage, at least part of the way, to use them.

Imagine you had a sales person who just brought you lists of people who they'd shook hands with. That's all they'd done. No conversation to understand who those people were and whether your business could help them. Why would they do that? I suspect it was because they didn't really know who they were fishing for so they just brought you everything. It's a long time since sales people were targeted on *volume over value*. The same should stand for marketing.

Let's return to the example of the marketing team who didn't know what their collateral, email campaigns, social posts and so on were about.

The reason I'd come in to lead the team was explicitly to *improve the marketing*. It became clear to me quickly that it was in fact to teach the organisation about marketing and to teach the marketing team about the business. Once I'd bridged that gap - using a marketing plan and some tools, templates and coaching (on both sides) the marketing started to work. And the team went from being the *under-performers* to the *star team*. A couple of people in the team I inherited changed, but in most cases it was the same people who were being described in this way.

If you isolate anyone they do one of two things; *fight you* or *withdraw*. Usually in that order. Then if they have anything about them, they'll leave. If they don't, they'll coast and blame everyone else for why they do that.

When I speak with potential clients I ask them about their marketing team or person and what behaviours they're seeing. The answers fall into two camps. *They keep doing things that we don't need (fight you)* or *They don't add any extra value, they just do what me or my sales person tell them (withdraw)*. In either camp that marketer is going to be disillusioned and demotivated.

Your marketer has a role all of their own in the organisation. Your job is to help them see where they fit and train and coach them on what's important to the business. Help them connect with the rest of the organisation and see each area of the business as a player they are *orchestrating* their marketing for.

I was at a marketing conference two years ago where I heard the phrase *Snapchat is not a strategy.* I laughed out loud, because the day before a fairly new marketer in my team had suggested that we needed to be on *Snapchat* as an organisation. When I asked them why they said, *Because it's the latest thing and everyone is on it now.* We targeted *Baby Boomers* and *Gen X CXOs* in global organisations. I suspected they weren't hanging out on *Snapchat.*

What this didn't tell me was *this marketer is no good.* It told me that I hadn't done my job well enough of helping them understand where to fish.

I'm not against social media. Far from it; you probably found this book via a social or digital post.

I *am* against *clicks* over *communication.*

In orchestral terms social posts might be the beat of the drums underneath the music. It's not a performance in its own right and you wouldn't expect it to be performed outside of the piece - but it is providing a rhythm that keeps everything going. Marketing is a whole performance. One that can build your brand if you let it.

Scaling a business is a whole new challenge from building it. It requires a degree of organisational change and the role you play will inevitably be different from that you played as founder or leader of a team of three or four people.

If you're reading this book and you lead a growing service business you're either an entrepreneur who likes to spot and respond to each opportunity, or you have exceptional technical expertise in your field and bring a reputation you could monetise. Critically, in either case, you have to be involved in all the moving parts to make sure it hangs together. Your team probably think that you personally are the value proposition or brand, and they have to mimic you to be successful. You may wonder why no one else can easily describe what you do.

There is a point in your business growth that this approach becomes infeasible. To scale your business more quickly, you can no longer be the individual glue. Your role moves from being composer to that of conductor - someone who doesn't play any of the instruments yourself. This can be a hard choice for a leader. But it is a necessary one.

You also have to choose your best niche - it's hard to scale disconnected opportunities and be able to explain them simply. You need to pick one position based on the core of the problem you solve for customers. And hang your hat on it. To be successful, and for your team to follow you also have to turn down projects that don't fit with that value proposition.

Jim Collins describes this as the *Hedgehog Concept* in *Good To Great,* Simon Sinek as the *Celery Test* in *Start With Why.* Seth Godin writes about the country vet who struggles valiantly to operate on a rabbit rather than say *we don't do rabbits* and let a small animal specialist do the work instead.

This can all be stressful because it can require a change in mindset and behaviour from everyone. You're used to having all the answers and everyone else is used to that too. MDs and CEOs I've worked with at this critical transition stage, especially in service businesses, feel that their organisation is starting to lack clarity. They say *no one can describe what we do.*

They also lack marketing capability or confidence, saying *we're not good at marketing* or *our marketing isn't working.* And they seem to spend all their time chasing people and money: *We don't have a clear pipeline* or *I feel like a team of one.*

If any of those phrases resonate then your business is probably at the right stage for this book.

I'd now ask you to spend a minute looking at what I've just said from your marketer's perspective (or if you don't have one, from the perspective of all the people who have a bit of the marketing puzzle bolted onto their role - an approach in itself that's an inhibitor to growth). To have a chance at doing marketing well, they need to be able to do five things:

1. Identify where you're trying to fish and what problem you want to solve - who should be in the audience?

2. Craft a clear distinctive story about what you do and why people should choose you - what's your number 1 hit song?

3. Understand how all the parts of the organisation fit into that story (the evidence of your story, particularly for a service business) - write a score so all the players know when to come in.

4. Make sure that all the people in your organisation can tell and contribute to that story (things like sales aids, employee on-boarding and recognition can help your employees live the brand) - rehearse the performance.

5. Execute campaigns that build awareness and drive leads that connect to your sales pipeline and activity - enable your players to perform.

If they're being asked to send out ad hoc emails for different products or post lots of different and even conflicting stories on social media (and/or you are), then they're focused on step 5. If steps 1-3 aren't clear first, and you're not ensuring step 4, they will fail and you will both feel like it's not working.

Marketers I meet in these businesses tell me they lack clarity on what it is they're trying to market, saying, *I don't know what we really do.* They fear they lack marketing capability *I can't get anything done* or *I never get to finish anything because the strategy changes so frequently.*

And they're disillusioned because what they're doing isn't working and they tell me that *nothing works* or *sales don't follow up on anything.*

Sound familiar?

If you recall what the MDs told me, you'll see that they're the *same* three problems: *Lack clarity, lack capability* and *lack connected pipeline.* You face the same problems but you need to play different roles in fixing them, together. And the fact you're at that stage means you're ready to scale.

In this situation big businesses hire an experienced Marketing Director. Smaller scaling businesses hire a consultant. Either way, as the leader of the business, and the person who knows the answers to many of the questions marketing will ask, you need to be involved.

This book is about one thing. Guiding you through those five steps that will build a brand position and marketing strategy that you can execute at scale.

The first step is shifting your view of your own role. In musical terms you have been the composer/conductor/orchestrator/lead violin and also dabbled in playing every part in the symphony orchestra.

It's time for you to stop playing, and even stop being composer for a while and focus on being the conductor. That's how you'll get your brand, marketing and sales to sing from the same hymn-sheet, stay in tune and fill the concert hall with people who will give you a standing ovation.

I chose to write this book because I found that using musical principles can lift you out of the specific detail of your business whilst building a marketing strategy. That helps you find an external perspective and also highlights the internal politics that might be getting in your way. When I'm working with clients to build their value propositions and marketing strategies, I use musical analogies to help them understand why it's necessary.

It's also more fun - for you, your team and your marketer. It can allow you to step outside of the day-to-day business and find common ground.

Let me explain. Imagine you go to a classical concert. The orchestra all arrive on stage individually and choose any seat they like on the stage. Some of them like Beethoven, some have a personal preference for Handel, some like more contemporary music so they choose a piece by Ligeti. They all start playing at different times and you can't conduct because they're all in a different time and speed. They are all meeting the objective of *play your part in a symphony concert* - but each is playing to their own personal agenda.

It sounds awful and definitely not what you composed!

So you start trying to play some of the instruments yourself to make it sound better. You're running around the stage playing small bits of each part or each piece, but it just adds to the noise. You know what you wanted to perform but it just isn't shining through. Because each part has very different instrumentation there are too many people on the stage. It's probably costing a lot to put this concert on and in some places there are people sitting doing nothing.

Eventually, the Beethoven people all find each other and move to sit together. Beethoven was what your business first played so they're the most experienced players. The Beethoven starts to dominate and the other pieces struggle to be heard - those that the audience today actually want to hear.

Meanwhile, your marketing person is asked to sell tickets for this concert. Each person has briefed him on their part and their piece. He now has to tell three different stories at the same time. Or he has to try and make sense of the whole with a very convoluted narrative - then *Tweet* it in 280 characters! He also has a limited budget and everyone needs to have *a bit of their part* included in the marketing plan, so it looks fair. Which means nothing gets traction.

He actually has a bigger problem. Who wants to come to this concert? The Beethoven people don't like Handel and hate Ligeti. Some of the Handel fans might suffer Beethoven but not Ligeti. Some might try Ligeti but don't like Beethoven. The Ligeti fans think they're coming to an avantgarde performance and they like lots of discord not harmony. It's a tough sell.

Of course I am outlining an extreme situation. But is there any truth in this scenario in terms of what's happening in your organisation? If you're struggling to choose where to focus your marketing and how to explain what you do, there might be a bit of this going on.

There are several reasons this scenario happens:

- You're trying to be everything to everyone. Your only target is revenue and you're going to apply your skills to anything you're asked for. You can never fill the hall with an audience that will applaud because you're not clear on who you really want to come.

- Maybe you're no longer clear on which song you really play. You started with a very simple melody when you built your business and you harmonised it beautifully with a few parts that you could control. It's now several tunes competing for the airwaves.

- It could be that you have a clear tune but you didn't write (or brief) the other parts in enough detail. It's now grown into lots of different melodies that it's hard to keep in tune. You don't have a score - which is what a composer uses to decide who plays what, when.

- If you have a score, did you rehearse it? When businesses launch digital products they usually test them. How did you test or rehearse your service? In musical terms did your players learn their part AND where their part fits with others? Or did you put them on the stage and hope it would just sound OK because they're good players?

- Maybe you're not targeting a whole performance that incentivises the value the customer wants from your service? Does your marketer know what the whole performance sounds like, and your customers want from it?

What you need to do, is *Orchestrate* your performance:

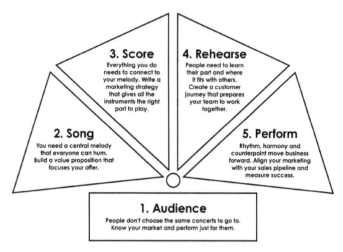

Thinking about your world and your challenges in this way, with your team, makes it less personal. Asking your team to write their song is more fun than asking them to construct a value proposition. Guiding them to make sure the score has the right amount of harmony and counterpoint in it and isn't dominated by one part is a good way to plan. Rehearsing the whole before asking them to learn their part off by heart will make sure it adds up. And aligning the goals of the performance to *getting a standing ovation* rather than *getting to the last note* will allow you to get the sound you want.

Involving your marketer through this process will allow them to bring your symphony to life. And attract the audience that your team all agree should be there.

Again, this book is about one thing. Guiding you through the five steps that will build a brand position and marketing strategy that you can execute at scale.

With *you* as conductor.

Chapter Two

WHY YOU NEED
A STRONG BRAND TO SCALE

I'm sure in your industry there's that over-simplification that you hate. In branding it's when someone says *Oh, you mean your logo?* They then talk about images, company names, colours and fonts. Of course these are important but they're not your brand. They're just a visual representation of it. A short cut.

Likewise in established service businesses. Your brand is no longer one person (you) and it's not your product. It might have started out as you being the product or brand - if you were selling your own expertise or time as a consultant - but it's now a lot more than that.

And needs to be.

So, why do you need a strong brand to grow your business?

Your brand is other people's perception of everything you do. The whole performance. If we return to the example of an orchestra on stage - from the minute someone sees the concert advertised, their interaction to buy the tickets, the tickets being received, their arrival at the concert hall, their seat, their programme, their interval drink, how you walk on stage, what you're all wearing, how the orchestra relates to their conductor, what you play, how well you play, how together you are, how you take the applause, the chatter as people leave the auditorium, the thank you or follow up email. All of these things are the brand. It's an experience. Even with a tangible product the packaging, ordering, delivery, returns process are part of the brand experience. Have you ever thought about it like that?

Here's the other thing to remember: **your brand exists in the mind of your potential and existing customers.** You can't control it. You can only influence it - steer that perception - by what you do. You are the *guardian* of the brand. You are not the brand.

In both the London orchestra and directory companies I worked for, I was lucky enough to sit behind the one-way glass in focus groups and hear what people said about our brands.

One way of getting them to articulate it unconsciously (and brutally) is to ask for an analogy. *If this business were a person/building/car/book/handbag - what would they be?*

I've heard a concert hall described as *Quasi Modo* and a sales business described as an ageing rusting brown *Rover.* Not what those businesses wanted to hear, but it was valuable feedback about how the whole performance was perceived. Of course you can then ask people why they say that - what is it that brand does, says, or looks like that makes them think or feel that. This allows you to get at the tangible stuff you can actually change.

A brand can really differentiate you. It can attract your tribe because people who like the same car that you want to be, are the people who will be easiest to influence to buy from you.

Seth Godin, marketing author and teacher phrases this as *people like us do things like these.*

One of the biggest challenges for scaling businesses is to focus where they fish. To be brave enough to turn business away. I referenced Seth's example before about the vet who *doesn't do rabbits,* trying to do so and taking five times longer (and therefore five times the cost) than a small animal specialist. When you start a business, especially if you're entrepreneurial by nature, it's all about taking different opportunities. Starting with Yes. Saying *No, I don't do that* feels like turning away a big opportunity.

I have the same challenge. People contact me and ask if I can run a social media campaign for them, send out an email or write some copy for a brochure. I could do it, but it would take a lot longer for me than a social media consultant or copy editor. I would cost more per hour than that specialist so the ROI on the campaign wouldn't make sense. And so I've learned to say *no.* I explain what I do and the ballpark cost and just the people who that most helps will say *yes.* I always get that insecure feeling of *turning money away,* but I also remember the feeling of saying *yes* and struggling to deliver.

Let me share a musical example. I trained as a singer and I sing in two choirs. One is a local community choir where most of the members have no musical training. The repertoire is a mix of well-known popular music and community folk songs from around the world. It's about introducing the joy of choral singing to a community. The other choir is one of the world's leading independent choruses - *The Bach Choir.* The audience (and singers') expectation is different and we perform in the top concert halls, with professional orchestras. It's about precision and nuance and pushing the standards of choral singing.

Both are mixed-voice choirs, yet their brand purpose is very different. They serve different segments. And so their approach to which songs they choose to sing, how many parts that encompasses, how they rehearse, what they perform, what they wear and how they expect the audience to behave are completely different. Other than my partner who has to attend both, they attract different audiences.

It's the same with corporate brands. *Apple* and *Microsoft* both sell tablets and computers. But they have very different tribes and in a brand perception test would be very different cars. My point is, *be true to your car.* Building on and playing to your strengths will win you better customers - people who you can really serve and help.

When I was 16, I took part in a local singing competition. Everyone who entered sang the same piece called *Song To The Seals.* Most of us knew each other and were taught by the same singing teacher. Of the girls singing, I didn't have the best voice - I lacked some power and technique over my rivals. But I won. This surprised most of them (and me). I won because the judge bought into what my brand brought. I didn't focus on being the best technically. I focused on telling the story of the broken-hearted girl singing to the seals in the ocean. I was therefore memorable and different to everyone else, and that was the brand of that song that that judge was looking for. Another judge, who was looking for technical superiority, would not have placed me first.

If I say I work in marketing rather than brands, people ask me about advertising (or these days social media) or getting leads. Of course, our reason for influencing people is to get them to do what we want (buy our product, read our book, donate to our cause, attend our concert).

But it's not all we're doing.

A need for marketing to prove its value leads junior marketers in execution roles to focus on counting things. Usually *clicks*.

Clicks are like applause. They come at the end of the performance. You definitely start with a desire for your audience to enjoy and appreciate your performance. But just counting the claps is one-dimensional. Not converting *clicks* into sales can become a very tense debate between marketing and sales - was the issue that the people who clicked were wrong or that sales didn't follow up well or quickly enough. Ever been in the middle of that?

Too often marketers aren't trained to focus on the whole performance. I think that this is the single biggest issue with how marketing works or doesn't. Targeting *clicks* alone isn't scalable and it's how marketing becomes disconnected from the rest of the business.

I worked for an executive learning organisation and when I joined, their social media focused predominantly on students. They sold to C-Level Executives so sales complained that marketing were wasting their time on the wrong audience. Marketing thought sales didn't understand social media which got better engagement from a younger audience. The issue was that the very junior marketing intern had no understanding of who the business targeted and how they made money. She therefore picked one aspect of what they did to focus on (a good marketing approach) but picked the one that interested her and she could relate to because she had recently left college. With a blank canvas and everyone telling her a different story about what the organisation did, she filled the void with what she knew.

Another reason to build a strong brand is that brands have tangible value.

Millward Brown specialises in measuring this for large organisations with their *BrandZ* ranking; in 2019 *Amazon's* brand is worth $315,505m. Research shows that those with a strong brand can charge significantly more for their service compared to a competitor with an unknown brand. Right now you will pay 70p for a tin of *Heinz* beans vs. 65p for *Branston* and 32p for the own-store variety.

If you run a business you already know this.

I had an interesting experience of this first hand when I worked for a small advisory company who was eventually acquired by a global advisory service. What they acquired wasn't really our product, but the affinity and involvement that C-Level customers had with our company. We had exceptional analysts whose expertise was coveted but what customers wanted was to be part of the cool club that other Global C-Levels were in. Our brand was about serving and facilitating those people to be who they wanted to be. And that increased the brand's value.

When you study marketing strategy you learn about *The Four Ps* that your strategy needs to cover. Originally there were four: *Product, Price, Place* and *Promotion*. In services marketing this was expanded to seven with three additions - *People, Process* and *Physical Evidence*.

Most people think of marketing just being about *Promotion*, and many businesses treat their marketer as the promotion person - asking them to send out emails or run events. There is a reason why this P comes last - because until you know what you're offering, to whom, what it costs, where they get it, how they experience it, who does what and how it all links together, you don't really know what you're promoting or how to promote it. Neither does your marketer.

In musical terms, if you don't know what your song is, who you're singing it to and why they want to hear it, you're probably just going to sing in the shower!

Your brand and its value proposition (the problem it solves and why that's good for your audience) are the positioning tools at the centre of the strategy. They are the guiding light for all you do and in strategic terms they are as important as your profit target. They give you something other than making money, to link your four or seven *Ps* to. Which products you create, how you price them, where they can be bought, how your team behave, what the process is like for the customer - all of these things need to be consistent with your value proposition to reinforce your brand.

Consider *IKEA* vs. *John Lewis*. *IKEA* is an interesting example of a different value proposition. They sell you a modern lifestyle (*The wonderful everyday*) at an affordable price, immediately. You don't have to wait two weeks for a delivery that involves you taking a half day off work.

To get that you have to do some of the work yourself. Well a lot of it really. They do the design work and let you experience which furniture combinations will realise your lifestyle. They also provide the physical parts of the furniture so handle the buying, sourcing and part of the manufacturing. But you become the process. A whole portion of their supply chain operations now sit with you. You get the stock off the shelves. You deliver. You assemble. You get a discount because you do part of the work. You're one of the employees as well as the customer.

Imagine the uproar in the Home Counties if *John Lewis* asked you to do this. If you've ever bought a self-assembly sofa from *John Lewis* it means the four feet might have to screwed on. They deliver quality, for a market-comparable price, that involves no work for you. They target older customers who are probably changing one piece of furniture, not building a whole room from scratch. They promise to give you this quality at a fair price matching like for like. Their people know their stuff and go out of the way to serve you. Their delivery van always arrives in the time slot they gave you and gives you a 30 minute warning before they arrive so you can pop home if you're out. You don't do anything and you pay for that privilege.

For both *IKEA* and *John Lewis*, the details back up their own promise and each of them stick to it. If you don't know what your promise is, or it's different for every customer (or you change it every month like a fad), you can't scale it. Not least because your employees can't build or deliver it. They never get time to optimise it to see if it really works before you've moved on.

The other challenge with a constantly changing value proposition is that it's hard to engage people in something if they're unclear on what it is. It's also hard to optimise processes and become efficient (and so be profitable). And if your employees are driven by more than money (which most are), they have to invent their own *why* in order to motivate themselves to get out of bed.

Your proposition and profit are dual targets and everything you choose to do should tick both boxes. Don't be tempted to trade-off, they are equally important. The marketing strategy is about finding the intersection of the two.

They say money makes the world go round. It also causes most conflicts in the world. They also say money can't buy you love. That includes brand-love. If the only target you give your employees, and therefore your brand, is money - you're scaling discord.

That's why you need a strong brand to help you scale.

Chapter Three

THE CHALLENGES OF SCALING

I recently asked a number of managing directors/business owners to tell me their top three problems.

- 21% of the time they mentioned cashflow and a lack of clarity across the business.

- 20% of the time they mentioned a lack of time and confidence in what they were doing, and;

- 18% of the time they talked about chasing people to get things done.

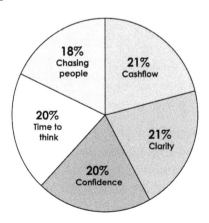

These were all scaling businesses and the word chasing came up time and time again.

As a new businesses you probably started out with a very clear vision of what you were trying to achieve. It might have been a gap in the market or a problem that no-one was solving. Even if it was just *doing what the big companies do better/without the bureaucracy* - there's a purpose to what you set out to do. It might also have appealed to you to take control. In a small business with a handful of employees you were the *system* or *process* that held everything together. Problem is, this becomes impractical.

Usually at around ten employees you either become the bottleneck so have to work every hour to keep things moving; or you control things so much no one wants to work for you because they can't learn or grow. Either way, it's not scalable.

I've been there. Both as a team leader - where as a marketing director with a team of 35 I had to learn how to delegate and get clear and specific on the desired outcome but leave the *how* to others. Then as an employee, where the MD would sit in the design team changing the colours or fonts to his preference; a part of my job became a human shield to keep him away from the team and out of the detail so they could do their jobs. We all want people to know what we've learned and avoid our mistakes. Ironically they won't learn if they can't make any! I still see this and perhaps you're guilty of one or the other? It comes back to choosing between being a player in the orchestra or the conductor.

As the MD/Founder of your business you have learned a lot of about what the market wants and become attuned to spotting real opportunities. Whether you're a serial entrepreneur or a brilliant technician in your field, you will enjoy creating things. This tends to lead to a desire to create more and more new products, which if done too fast, can be hard to follow or market.

It's important to innovate. Let's return to the orchestra on stage. If they played exactly the same tune for 20 years, the audience would get bored and so would the orchestra. So from time to time they add a new *product* or piece to their repertoire. But the good ones are careful to keep that repertoire tight and connected. They introduce their audience to something similar, or a progression of the Beethoven symphony they love. It's easier for the audience and means the players understand why they're playing it without explanation.

If you're launching products to cover every possible base, every type of customer, and telling your team that they are all equally important, you're effectively building a game of *whack-a-mole!*

Last year, I worked with a couple of very different clients with similar challenges. They both had the same root cause to their problems; they needed to pick a clear song and write the score so that their teams could learn their parts and play it. They had both fallen into the trap of trying to be all things to all people.

One of them continually refused to be pinned down, despite my, and her leadership team's best efforts. She was unable to see that the reason no one could explain what they did was because she wouldn't let them. She'd say in one breath *we're business consultants* only to launch a data-centre service the following day. Consequently she hasn't launched the proposition that her team and I built and I doubt she ever will. It's the musical equivalent of expecting the players to switch pieces half way through the performance. No one ever gets to the end and few people enjoy that.

The other listened to the client insight and potential directions that I presented. He bought into the concept of picking one song and actually wrote most of the proposition himself. We led workshops with his team to begin the *Orchestration* process and re-align what people were developing or delivering to their proposition and then I stepped away. Last week I saw his proposition on Underground posters and bus sides.

This is a common challenge. People often want to change their brand before it's fully embedded (because they're bored with it and make the mistake of assuming that their customers have seen it as much as them). Similarly, it's easy to think launching another product is the answer to cashflow, when building processes to get more or quicker revenue from your existing products might be better use of your time. New products rarely make money from the off.

In these types of businesses marketing is often seen as tactical. And that's actually one of the biggest symptoms and causes of your lack of clarity, and your lack of marketing capability.

You can tell if that's where you are because your marketer will be sending out emails that other people have written (or you rewrite constantly). They are seen by others as the *make it look nice* team. As you know, what then happens is the marketer has less and less incentive to engage and feels more and more disconnected. In a recent survey I asked marketers and MDs to say if their marketing felt like a joined-up, orchestrated brand performance. The marketers were more than twice as likely to say no than the MDs.

I remember joining one large organisation and inheriting a small marketing team. In my first week, they had some client facing slides that needed sign-off from the Director (my new boss).

There was a lot of chatter about images needing to be blue and when I enquired why, the answer was *He signed if off when we made it blue last time.* They were second-guessing what would get signed off. Rather than thinking about what worked well for the brochure, or engaged the customer. At the end of the week I led a session with the marketing team where we put an example of every piece of collateral, email, recent press releases on the table. And then asked *what's its purpose?* Both for the client - what are they supposed to get from it and what's the next step we're asking them to take. And for us, the organisation; who will use it, how and when. In many cases they didn't know and once I'd reassured them that I didn't blame them for that, we had a good healthy discussion about how we thought it should work. And how to collect the information on what was really needed.

It's a good exercise to run - I'd recommend you try it. It's rare that it's all joined up and usually it's a clear signal that lots of parts of the organisation are demanding their own thing, and the marketer is trying to *cover all bases so everyone gets something.* It comes from a protection mindset, which won't help you grow. And it's not great for your brand either.

Two of the people I refer to above were experienced marketers who just needed someone to help them say no to random requests for a while - so they had space to build a suite of marketing materials that actually helped. The third was very junior and so didn't know enough to challenge it. In smaller, scaling organisations, there's often a talented but inexperienced marketer trying to navigate this phenomenon. They are usually excellent at executing but they've not yet had the business experience to ask the questions that would connect their strategy to what the organisation really does and the commercial outcomes required. They become reactive to what they're asked to do, and obsess on *clicks* so they can feel valued, and the cycle begins. After a while, if they're any good, they leave in search of what they need to succeed. I wonder if this is in-part responsible for job mobility being famously high in marketing.

Whenever I start working with a new organisation I go out and ask a range of employees what they do. And where they fit. Often when I ask them what they do they tell me what I should do - what marketing they need. I have to work hard to get to what they do, how that helps customers and what their perceptions of the organisation are.

In this scenario, I'm actually trying to assess how *in tune* the players are. I have learned how to do that as a first step to getting towards a clear audience and a more coherent symphony to play. Before marketing even considers inviting anyone to listen.

One of the signals I listen out for when I'm deciding whether to work with a new client, is how they talk about their marketer. They often say that their marketing isn't working and that their marketer isn't doing the right things. They're often unsure what to do about this other than dive in and micro-manage.

When I start working with the client, their marketer is equally unhappy. They can't understand what they're being asked to do (and often even what the company really does) and so they can't link marketing to the business.

The journey I work through is a way of helping you both learn how to connect those dots. Constantly telling your marketer *'We do this'* doesn't work; they need to be part of the process to uncover it.

To focus your brand, and especially if you then want to scale, you need something other than yourself that will provide some direction and control. You need a clear song - or value proposition. You need a score - something that helps all of your people play or explain it the same way. And you may need to shift your own leadership approach to keep the focus on your symphony.

Simon Sinek calls this the *Celery Test*. If you say you're about celery and yet your team constantly see you putting cookies, chocolate, crisps and lemonade in your shopping cart they won't believe you.

Daniel Priestley, founder of the *Key Person of Influence* programme, says "Your team are not your therapist. You can't keep trying out a new idea every day with them. You need to keep them consistently focused on what's important today until you're really sure that something else is really going to be better.".

If you're conducting a Beethoven symphony and that's what you've advertised, then that's what you should play in that concert. If you suddenly start conducting a Schubert concerto some of the orchestra start playing Schubert, some keep playing Beethoven, and quite a few stop, look around and ask, *What are we playing now?* The audience is wondering what they booked for but essentially they get to hear neither.

In this situation what is the marketer supposed to promote? And what do they do on the night when this happens?

Of course, I'm being obtuse to make a point. But it only takes a few players out of tune, or playing a different piece, before the performance grinds to a halt and the orchestra leaves. Players play out of tune and singers sing out of tune for a few reasons. They may be singing the wrong song, they may have the music for the wrong part of that song, they may be an inexperienced singer and need more rehearsal, they may be a cellist not a singer. Most of all they're not listening to (or can't hear) the whole. And perhaps neither are you.

It's your job to keep them listening. To point out where it's out of tune, diagnose why and help them fix it. And to train them how to listen for themselves.

As the conductor, you should never turn around, face the audience and sing yourself.

The challenges of scaling are about both your marketing and your leadership. And thinking like a musician can help.

Chapter Four

WHAT YOU CAN LEARN FROM A SYMPHONY

For all the brilliance of the composer, what creates the symphony, the proof of its endurance, is the performance. In Lucca, Italy I got to see some pages of Puccini's operatic scores and it was amazing to see *Tosca* orchestrated line by line. But if I hadn't heard the music itself it would have been less impressive.

What *Tosca* means to me is essentially an emotional reaction. And my reaction to *Tosca* is different from yours. I love *Tosca* because I heard a bunch of musicians play and sing it at a particular time.

It's about the performance, not the notes.

One of the common challenges for service businesses, especially those with complex, technical and intangible aspects to their service, is how to talk about the whole. *We can't explain what we do* is a challenge I'm often posed with. When I've joined organisations as Marketing Director I often ask sales to tell me what their solution does for clients. It's not long before I hear *It's different for every client.* They then go into a number of features of their product. The product development team (often analysts or developers) love to show you how brilliant and complicated the detailed features are - because they're rightly proud of that work. But imagine if *Google* tried to explain their algorithm before they'd give you the search result!

It's very common for companies to focus on the features not the benefits of their service because that's usually the source of their IP and differentiation.

I remember having an interview for a job where the guy who would later be my boss put a glass of water in front of me and asked me to tell him what the *features* and *benefits* were.

I now use that myself - not only when hiring marketers but also when trying to get my clients to shift from features to benefits. Try it with your team. People will tell you things like it's clear, it's cold, it's smooth (describing the glass) and then they'll say it holds water as the benefit. I rarely get up in the morning and think about finding something to hold water. I wake up and think I'm thirsty and the problem I'm solving is a need to quench my thirst. That's a *benefit*.

I'd argue you could even go further. It's proven that drinking lots of water keeps you healthy - remember *Evian's* campaign featuring babies - *Evian: Live Young*. If I believed what I read in *Marie Claire*, drinking more water might even lead me to look like Kate Moss. The benefit is good health.

The marketing lesson here is that you need to talk in benefits first, not features. The musical point is that it's about the performance, and what that does for your audience, not the notes. But you can't get to one without the other.

If you grew up in the UK in the times of Vaudeville, you'd have seen the one-man band performer on stage. This was a man whose feet played the drum, knees played the symbols, lips played the mouth-organ, and had another instrument in each hand. This is what it's like when you start off in business as a sole trader. It's an amazing testament to their founders that these businesses survive.

If you went to watch an orchestral concert, you'd find it very strange if the conductor kept leaping off the podium and playing someone's instrument for them. Equally, very few people can play more than one instrument well, but if they do, they don't attempt to do it simultaneously.

Each instrument actually has a different sound. A different texture to add and a different role to play in the soundscape. The composer respects that. When she writes the score, which part of the orchestra gets to play which bit is an important consideration. The same tune played by a trumpet or a cello will sound very different. These different instruments are built to work together to create a collective sound, and it's the overall sound that the audience are buying.

A symphony is a collective experience. One of the things I most learned from playing in bands and orchestras or singing in choirs, is the discipline to respect my own part and where it fits in the collective sound. I also learned you have full rehearsals, sectional rehearsals and individual practice. What order you do these in depends on the skill level of the team.

I sing in *The Bach Choir* - London's oldest independent chorus. All the singers can sight read well and many have been in the choir for years. The first rehearsal of a new piece is normally a sing through. This allows the conductor and the individual singers to understand the areas that need work. Right from the off I'm clear on the whole that I'm contributing to. It's not about me. It's about a choral performance that my voice contributes to.

I then have to go away and undertake individual practice on the bits I found more difficult. And in the next rehearsal our conductor will zone in on particular sections, part by part. He's heard the bit the altos are finding hard or the tenors are finding tricky. So he gives them the forum to focus on just their part and then hear it fit back into the whole.

I also sing in a local community choir called *Vocality*. Here there are inexperienced singers and we don't get given a score as most people can't read music. Instead we practice from recordings broken out into individual parts and then a summary track. The collective learning process is usually different - each part is taught a couple of phrases and then hears how it sounds to sing all the parts together. Whilst the process of building to that is opposite, the anchor is still the whole piece, and hearing the collective sound is the achievement.

In your organisation, how much time do you devote to people experiencing the whole. Not only getting a sense of the end-to-end process and the baton-passes, but also what that's like from a customer seat? We all remember the advent of the IVR phone system and being passed from pillar to post for a simple enquiry, or never getting past *Press 16 for even more options!* How do you mitigate for this kind of experience in your organisation? Do you help your team experience it all or just assume they can join the dots for themselves?

When you're learning something new, it's very easy to rely on the strongest singers to carry everyone else. That can also be dangerous - what do you do if someone is sick or leaves just before the performance? In a musical team, individuals also have to take responsibility for their own part. In *The Bach Choir* one of the ways the conductor achieves this is to jumble us up. For some rehearsals or even concerts, we can't sit next to anyone who is singing the same part. This is actually quite liberating - I have to step up and understand very quickly what I don't know well enough and have to practice more. This isn't throwing someone in the deep end though; it's not usually in the first rehearsal that this happens.

Here's an exercise you can try with your team, that Sally Duncan uses as a warm-up at *Vocality* choir rehearsals. Break your team into two groups. First teach everyone to sing *Swing Low, Sweet Chariot.* Then to sing *Oh When The Saints Go Marching In.*

Next, get Team 1 to sing one of these at the same time as Team 2 sings the other. As long as you start on the same note pitch-wise, these songs fit together. Do it a couple of times until they're confident holding their own against each other.

Now finally, get everyone to stick to their own part, but walk around the room in any direction individually. Let them weave between each other. They will sometimes walk past someone singing the same tune, sometimes different. They suddenly can't rely on the person next to them to keep them in place. They are individually responsible for the collective sound.

For marketing to work, everyone needs to take individual responsibility. First, they need clear direction on what to sing.

Imagine if a choir arrived on stage at the *Royal Festival Hall* and you've come along to hear Bach's *St Matthew Passion.* What happens however, is that each singer decides to sing something a bit different. Because they're *innovative.*

What would you hear?

In business terms this indicates a lack of leadership or clear vision.

What if, instead, people form small groups on stage. And each group or section sings a different piece. It would be less discordant than the above example but it still wouldn't sound like Bach.

In business terms this is a siloed organisation. As a marketing director one of my biggest challenges has been resourcing marketing for silos. It often leads to a *bit of everything* strategy to minimise complaints from each department, rather than a focused big-bet strategy that will cut through.

The conductor programmes the music to attract a particular audience. They also guide the interpretation of that music - their own *take* on it. Are some sections slower or louder than another orchestra's performance? Before we start rehearsing a new piece in a choir we're often given *markings* that we need to put in our individual scores before the first rehearsal. This is where the conductor has already made some decisions about specific nuances he wants everyone to be aware of. Come off a beat early to make sure everyone can breathe. Don't breathe in the middle of this phrase. Sing this phrase very quiet. These markings make it easier to keep everyone together. Not only are they reading from the same score but they are also aware of the *specific way we do things here* that make our performance distinctive.

The final point to learn from a symphony is that *the audience decides whether it's a great performance or not.*

Just like your customers decide whether you're a great brand or not. And whether you have solved their problem or not. Some conductors of Beethoven will play up the drama by playing with the tempos and dynamics. Some will emphasise the original tempo to the letter. The same pieces will create different moods which will appeal to different people.

Over one Christmas I watched a lot of the *Bond* movies and I noticed a distinct difference in the way the *Bond* theme is orchestrated (what instruments are used, what dynamics, what tempo) in a Sean Connery vs. Roger Moore vs.Daniel Craig *Bond* movie. The same very famous tune has a different *feel* to match that actor's take on *Bond*.

I mentioned at the start of this book that as a 12-year old, I was in a choir that won a televised competition. I distinctly remember a conversation with our conductor on the coach home from the quarter finals asking, *"Will we win?"* She laughed and said it was unlikely. Her focus wasn't on winning. Her focus was on us giving our performance and showing our own blend of excellence.

The audience, the judges, decided we were award-winning; not us - and so *your audience will decide if you have a winning brand.* It exists in their mind and it's shaped by how well orchestrated and conducted it is at every point they experience it. Together, you and your marketer need to map that out and decide which bits to emphasise. That will also allow your marketer to focus on which points to promote, which emails or social posts to create and who to engage with them.

It's not rocket science. It's brand music.

Chapter Five

THE POWER OF ORCHESTRATION

So, what is *orchestration?*

If you type orchestration into *Google* its definition is:

1. *The arrangement or scoring of music for orchestral performance, and*

2. *The planning or coordination of the elements of a situation to produce a desired effect, especially surreptitiously.*

This last word is actually quite important. You are creating an effect from the component parts. It's not always tangible. This is great news for a service business that often deals in intangible products and services. If you get good at orchestration customers will better value your brand without needing to know why. We all have examples of companies we use or buy from who we just *like.* Everything they do seems good, even the way they handle complaints. They're on it.

Somewhere someone has *orchestrated* that.

In music, sometimes the composer themselves does the orchestration. In writing their symphonies Beethoven and

Mozart scored out all the parts to their melody, movement by movement.

Sometimes someone else orchestrates. For example, Thomas Tallis wrote a chorale in 1567 that Vaughan Williams orchestrated into the *Fantasia on a Theme by Thomas Tallis* in 1910. Tallis wrote his original piece of music before the symphony orchestra was even invented.

You have already been orchestrating. If you grew from being one person to four people, you divided jobs between parts. What you might not have done though, is looked at how that *sounded* from the customers perspective. Most likely you were the personal glue holding that together. The audience thinks it's just you and doesn't ever see the people behind you. There's a size you get your business to where this doesn't work.

I've developed five principles of orchestration to help you build your marketing strategy and brand. The foundation is *write and score it for a specific audience.* There are four more steps you need to work through: a clear song, a planned score, a rehearsal schedule and a consistent performance.

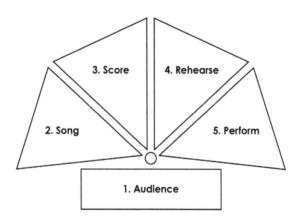

A symptom of not having a clear audience is that an organisation tends to talk only about themselves. All their social posts start with *We....* - in the absence of a person to address. Ask yourself this question - how much time do you spend at a party with someone who talks only about themselves - the *pins you in a corner and lectures* type? Not long, if you're lucky! How would you feel if you bumped into them at another party? I doubt you'd seek them out for more.

In musical terms you can't programme your concert unless you know who might attend. In the next chapter we'll look at how to narrow your audience.

A key solution is to get a clear view of the problems you really solve and pick the one or two you want to focus in on. This is always the starting point for a marketing campaign. My partner and I would choose very different gigs to attend - he likes 80s Synths or Bach, I like 70s disco or Vaughan Williams. He likes structure, I like emotion.

If you don't have a clear *song* or melody that you own, and that everyone in your organisation can sing, then you have nothing to hang all the parts on. If one of your challenges is that no one in your organisation can describe what you do, or everyone describes it slightly differently, this could be your problem. Sometimes this comes from an unclear audience or too many audiences competing for airtime. In Chapter 7, we'll look at how to get to a clear song by building a value proposition. Something sales people are often better at than marketers.

In music, the *score* guides people to play the right part at the right time. Just as we've shared the scenario of an orchestra coming to the stage and playing different pieces, imagine selling someone a product which they may or may not be able to use; leaving it to chance. Without a score your marketing has nothing to guide what it supports and drives. Usually in this scenario every department is unhappy with marketing. And believe me, that's no fun for them. In Chapter 8 we'll talk through the elements of a strategic marketing plan and building a marketing calendar.

Rehearsals allow people to learn and develop. Part of that is also helping them understand where they fit. It's routine to user- and technically- test products before they're released. You have Beta versions but even these would be prior tested to make sure they at least fulfil their core purpose. Services are often under-rehearsed and slowly become a collection of workarounds. If your team feel like they're not able to use their correct skills or aren't set up to help people (internally or externally) then this could be your problem. For your marketer it's better to give them time to get one part working before they amplify it. In Chapter 9, I will share some tips for rehearsing efficiently.

And finally the *performance*. Consistency is key. A simple way to spot this is to see how consistent everyone's email signature is. It also tells me the organisation's tolerance for being consistent. Consistency is important to marketing because with most services it's not as simple as you advertise what you have, people click and then they buy. They will come to you via a range of actions and interactions with you and your content. If that isn't consistent you lose them before they even decide to speak with you.

Whilst marketing is not sales' servant, marketing does need to assist sales. I remember working with a brilliant Chief Commercial Officer who was leading sales in a 60-employee company. In his first company-wide meeting he gave everyone a sticker as they entered the room. It said, *I'm a member of the sales team*. Some people wore it with pride, others hated the idea - but through his presentation it became clear that he wasn't asking everyone to go out and cold-call. He was asking them to connect the dots back to its impact on customer acquisition and retention and evaluate their work through that lens. How would people in your business feel if you did that, and what does that tell you?

Orchestration of this takes a bit of time and thought. But it doesn't have to be onerous and using musical principles can make it less political. The payoff is that everyone can contribute and the audience gets what they expect. Which for you means happy customers - and more revenue.

In the *Brand Symphony* everyone is part of the sales team. Because it's *one* performance you're selling.

SECTION 2

THE ORCHESTRATE METHOD

THE BRAND SYMPHONY

Chapter Six

AUDIENCE

When you pitch to a potential new customer, you tailor what you say to them. It's the same principle for your website. If it's not clear who it's talking to, then you're talking to no one in particular. Which tends to lead you to be very factual in what you say, or so creative no one can tell what you do. You need to have your ideal customer in mind and talk *to* them.

Your website and your brochure are part of a longer conversation with them. We buy from people we trust and to trust you, people have to know you. They get to know you from all the interactions they can have with you before you meet. They will engage if you talk to them directly.

Many classical composers like Haydn, Mozart or Beethoven were actually employed by a court; a wealthy patron. They were writing ostensibly for one person. You may be thinking: *But we serve lots of different types of customers.* Of course you do; so do I. But whether they're financial analysts, supply chain leaders, nuclear physicists, HR consultants or business change experts, they all speak with me because they have a few common problems that I help them solve.

The first step I work through with them is to get to the bottom of what problems they are really solving for *their* clients.

This is the same principle as programming a musical concert. People don't choose to go to the same concerts because they like different things. Their reasons for being there might be different (some are there to *collect* a performance, some are there to give their brain a night off, some are there to be seen, some are there to connect with friends). What they have in common is that they preferred Beethoven to the Stravinsky concert down the road. A key principle of concert programming is that all the pieces need to work together. People are buying the whole performance not just one piece.

My neighbour and I went to *Glyndebourne* last year. We settled on Janáček. She would have chosen Handel or Monteverdi (Baroque period music, quite structured). I would have chosen Mussorgsky or Puccini (Romantic period plenty of emotion). Janáček was a good compromise between the two - something that had musical elements we both liked - otherwise we would have been bored.

Why play to an audience that's bored? Or interested in only a third of what you do for them. It would be very strange to programme a combination of Ligeti, Beethoven and Delius in the same concert. You could think that you'll attract people interested in all three - so you broaden your audience. What actually happens is people who love each are put off. Unless your proposition is *come and try classical music for the first time and figure out which you like best* (the musical equivalent of a *Harvester* all you can eat buffet). Even a taster menu in a restaurant is planned to make sure that one course doesn't fight with another.

You need to build packages of like-minded repertoire.

When I worked for a London orchestra I was in charge of sales and marketing. There were many regular subscribers and after a few years I knew which specific people would be attracted by which repertoire. I could second guess their booking forms, so when I was writing copy to advertise that concert I had specific people in mind. It helped that the concerts team programmed repertoire that made sense together. Different concerts appealed to different people but all of them showcased our *unique selling proposition (USP)* - a rich, warm string sound.

At *Thomson Local,* the directory company I mentioned earlier, we started to build local advertising packages according to what drove a small business to buy. Some cared about local presence - being seen in the local area across lots of media - bus sides, *Google* and display ads. Some just wanted *clicks* and leads, especially if they weren't interested in building long-term affinity. Each package was built and marketed with someone specific in mind.

A brilliant charity in the UK called *Modern Muse,* empowers young girls to learn business leadership skills from women business leaders. The funding for this comes from corporate organisations. For some of those organisations it's part of their corporate responsibility charter, yet for others it's about training their own female leaders, or the grass roots work to start addressing gender diversity. Each has different drivers and the benefits they expect, and so the most important features, are different.

The *Audience* step in *The Orchestrate Method* is figuring out what problems you're really solving and then prioritising which of those you're going to focus on. Too many and you're back to being all things to all people, and nothing specific to anyone; too few and you can't grow or diversify.

The first step is to figure out which tunes people will and

won't listen to and, importantly, why. What's driving them to buy from you? There are three areas to understand in order to do this well:

a. Establish how consistent you are now.

b. Understand why and how others are connecting with you - logically and emotionally.

c. Ask where they'd go or what they'd do if you didn't exist.

Armed with this information you can start to look for common patterns and traits amongst your customers. You can then choose which problems you really want to solve, and finally draw your customer (yes, I'm going to get you drawing!)

Ideally you would do this with your marketer and maybe a couple of other key stakeholders. If you can let your marketer do some of the info gathering or facilitate some of these sessions, it will give them the involvement and platform they need to do their job well moving forwards.

STEP 1: CONSISTENCY REVIEW

Let's start by reviewing what you're currently saying across everything. You could do this by getting all your current materials out on a table or wall. Or pin them all onto one online mood board if you have a big screen. Make sure you don't just have marketing collateral. What about your customer service emails, your welcome pack or invoice? What does your receptionist says when he or she picks up the phone?

Now get some *Post-its* and try to summarise the key message in each piece of collateral in one sentence starting with we and a verb; *We do ... , We are...* e.g. *We do branding. We are mentors.*

Also for each, note what mood they evoke. Look at it and ask yourself *what's it feel like?* Which parallel services are you reminded you of? Some sites might remind you of an online magazine, some a technical manual, some a healthcare company, some a facilities company.

You will already start to spot inconsistencies but resist the urge to start changing them. DO NOT start running around the office *tweaking*. It will be a very unproductive and disruptive exercise until you know what you're going to align all your messages to. All you will do is confuse everyone further.

At the end of this exercise try and group your *We do Post-its* into broad categories. And then align the materials to them. Take a photo and ask your marketer to summarise the *We Do's*. Some of them will eventually make great campaign content.

This first step will give you a good idea of what your audience needs and wants. Or at least what you are *currently* pitching to.

STEP 2: DIRECT CUSTOMER INSIGHT

Next up you need to test this and understand why and how people are connecting with you. This is the most important step of this whole book. It can also be the hardest logistically because you need to schedule calls, meetings and surveys.

Yet it's vital you don't skip this step because it gives you the outside-in view of the song you need to sing.

Your customers will love the fact that you want their feed back so don't be afraid to ask them. You can use someone external to get an independent perspective, or your marketer can do it. Whoever does it needs to explain that you just want to understand their view of your strengths, weaknesses and what you do for them.

What you're trying to understand is:

i. What category they place you in. For example, *am I a marketing consultant or an agency, an interim CMO or a training programme?* How would they complete the sentence: *<BrandName is a.......>*

ii. What problem you solve for them. Ask them: *what job did you hire us to do?* Why is that important to them? What's the benefit of you solving that problem for them?

iii. How they feel about you. Here you need to ask them questions about the personality of your business. *What's common about your people, positive and negative?* It might even be worth asking them for an analogy. *If you were a pop band which band would you be and why?* Ask them which three words they most associate with your company; it's a great way to understand the language and words they prefer to use.

iv. Where they would go if you didn't exist. Often your customers don't want to tell you who they see as your competitors or bad mouth them. But if you ask them, *if we didn't exist what would you have done to solve your problem* you'll get a sense of what they are comparing you to. Sometimes it might just be we'd have done it ourselves rather than naming a competitor. Once you know this you can ask what you bring that's better and worse than the other solutions. This is important. If you are being compared to a bigger competitor your value proposition will need to play to your strengths vs. that competitor. If you are being compared to the customer doing it themselves, or using a piece of technology, your value proposition will need to play to those strengths instead. Don't assume your competition is who you think it is.

If someone is coming to see a symphony orchestra because it's film music, the competition might be films, not other symphony concerts. If it's about a night out it could be theatre. If it's about a particular piece or composer your competition could be a very good CD.

STEP 3: COMPETITIVE SET

Go and look at the websites of each of your competitors. What's their lead message? *We are... We do...*

What language do they use? Do they talk directly to someone or do they describe everything in the third person. What's the imagery and what emotions are they appealing to. Can you tell what problem they are promising to solve? If you printed off their and your statements - could you tell who was who?

Once you have this information you need to meet with your team and review it.

I can suggest two exercises to keep you focused:

1. List the alternative solutions and for each, say how you're the same, how you're better and what they offer that's better than you.

2. Draw a person in the middle of a large whiteboard or piece of paper. And write the words *Which me?* at the top. Now try and group your competitors based on which me they're targeting.

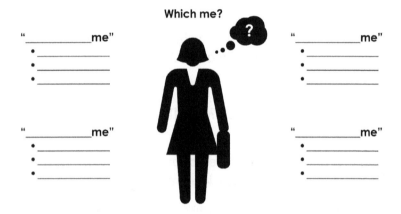

I'll give you an example: If you were a gym, you might target the healthy me and all your messages would be about improving my health. You might target the vain me and all your messages would be about how I'll look when I'm fit. You might target the practical me and all your messages would be about how easy it is to workout. Different gyms will target different *Me's*.

STEP 4: NAME YOUR IDEAL CUSTOMER

Ask your team to describe what makes an ideal customer *ideal*. Get them to describe a real person, and explore what their industry is, the problem they bring you to solve, the mindset they have, the size or structure of their company and any common traits that make them a successful customer for you to serve.

For our *Brand Orchestration Programme* I know that the most successful customers - the ones I can add real value to - are service businesses with about 10-50 employees and £2-7m turnover. They have at least one person in their business who is executing marketing (since someone inside the organisation needs to implement campaigns and drive momentum day in, day out). The single biggest factor of success however, is the mindset of the MD or CEO. If they don't want to change their approach or won't focus the company or give others clarity and consistency to deliver - then it won't work.

I reached this conclusion by looking at the traits of the past customers that had been less successful - in smaller companies without an in-house marketer there was no one to keep the programme going and in larger organisations there were too many conductors for marketing to orchestrate.

You could also ask your team which customers are the hardest to service and why. Are there common traits?

Take a piece of paper. Write *Best Customer* at the top, then for each complete these sentences briefly:

- *They do ...*
- *We do ...*
- *It works because ...*
- *It feels ...*

Once you have this, you will be in a much stronger position to define your audience fully and build your value proposition for them. You can't write, orchestrate or perform your symphony until you know who you're writing for.

STEP 5: WHO YOU SERVE (AND DON'T)

Together with your team, complete the following:

- We serve *<traits of the person>*
- Who want to *<what they want to achieve>*
- Which is important to them because they can *<benefit of what you do>*

Then:

- We don't serve *<traits of people who don't make good customers>*
- Who want to *<what they want to achieve that you're not going to offer>*

- Which is important to them because they can *<why they need it>*

- We're not the best people to do that because *<your or their weaknesses>*

- They would be better going to *<if they call up where will you refer them>*

Definitely pin this up in your office and see what comments you get from your team.

STEP 6: AUDIENCE INSIGHTS SUMMARY

The final step of this process is to summarise the key insights in a deck, as this process of summarising will bring clarity and help you simplify. You can download an outline deck here:

brandsymphonymarketing.com/tools

It covers:

- What problems customers want us to solve

- Which we're best placed to solve and will focus on

- How we're perceived by clients

- How we're perceived by staff and why that is different

- Who or what we're compared to

- What our strengths are vs. those alternatives

- What people want that we don't do (well)

Once completed you need to present this to your team and get their feedback. Ask them what pleases them, what surprises them, what they'd like to keep and what they'd like to change and why that's important to the audience (not just them).

STEP 7: DRAW YOUR CUSTOMER

Write down the details of your ideal customer and the problems you will focus on solving for them. Give them a name and draw them (I did say I'd make you draw!).

Our Customer

Does: _____   Doesn't: _____

Will: _____   Won't: _____

Says: _____   Won't say: _____

Wears: _____   Doesn't wear: _____

Visit: _____   Won't be found in: _____

Pin him or her on your wall.

You're now ready to write your song (your value proposition). Just for them.

Chapter Seven

SONG

Unless they're written to be sung simultaneously, we can generally only listen to one song at a time. Your business needs one central melody that everyone can hum and you need to relate it to your audience.

When you learn to read music you use rhymes to remember the letters for the notes on each line or stave. I now use this with businesses to help them remember the power of focus:

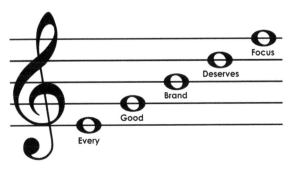

Organisations often use *Visions* or *Missions* to align people and they are helpful in providing an overall direction. Having launched many of these I can tell you that the biggest challenge in getting traction is belief, and the biggest challenge in driving belief is helping people connect what they do day-to-day with an aspirational vision. If there's dissonance between the day job and the vision, everyone continues focusing on the day job and nothing changes. Everyone continues singing their own song, even if it's out of tune with the brand. If you're unlucky, they'll all just sing louder but still in discord.

I first learned about building value propositions from sales. Sales use a value proposition to make sure that what they're offering actually solves a problem the customer is interested in. It's more externally focused than a vision or mission, and it's also more detailed. It covers why, what AND how and also articulates how your offering is different to the alternatives. It also focuses heavily on the benefits to the customer and less on listing every feature.

In musical terms it's the difference between writing a song only you want to sing and writing a song that your audience can hum along to. The latter will feel more enjoyable to your audience and spread the word more quickly

An organisational value proposition is a more practical guiding star, that can be used in conjunction with revenue or profit targets to guide decisions.

I firmly believe you get what you target, and if you target only revenue or profit, you will get behaviour that focuses on selling to anyone or cutting corners to improve margin. If you add a value proposition as a counter-balance to these measures - your team will focus on how to get more revenue and profit from customers you want.

The other advantage of a value proposition is that whilst it brings focus on who you want to do business with, there is some flexibility around the features that might deliver those benefits.

Sales people never build value propositions that are so rigid it becomes a needle in a haystack exercise to find a buyer!

Just like *The Bach Choir* don't do pop songs, and *Rock Choir* don't do four-part choral masses, other organisations who have strong value propositions have removed product lines that don't meet its values. Part of *Patagonia's* value proposition is to protect the planet we live on. In 2019, they actually stopped selling their power vest to certain companies who didn't align with their value proposition (whose businesses they deemed damaging to the environment). They felt the overall damage to the customer benefits they promised was greater than the short-term revenue/profit loss.

In *Good to Great,* Jim Collins calls this the *Hedgehog Concept*: "The *Hedgehog Concept* comes from the Greek fable about the fox and the hedgehog: while the wily fox knows many things, the simple hedgehog only knows one thing, but that one knowledge bit is highly impactful in protecting itself from danger. Discovering that simple but essential element is what created the success of the good-to-great companies."

He gives countless examples of what makes an organisation not just good but great - and part of what elevates them is a refusal to sell for revenue at the expense of their value proposition. I already shared Seth Godin's example of the poor vet struggling to save the rabbit with the wrong equipment in Chapter 1.

Just like a song is not a one-phrase jingle, a value proposition is not a tagline. You may develop a tagline once you have your value proposition, but focusing on finding a snappy phrase at this stage will stop you fully articulating the value. It's likely first off you'll write three or four value propositions before you pick the one you want to focus on. That's OK. In fact, it's good as it helps you find the one that will be the most compelling.

The first sentence is to state who it is you are serving. This tells your organisation where to fish. The first line of my value proposition is, *For MDs of service businesses with 10-50 employees and £2-7 million revenue.* It's broad enough that there's a market of more than one to go after but it's specific enough that I can get under the skin of their problems.

People often ask me why I don't work with smaller or bigger companies, since the principles of a value proposition are the same.

I have learned that new companies don't know enough about who they don't want to target, and the real problems they solve, to narrow their focus. They're in *explore mode.* And if they don't have at least one marketer in their organisation (someone 100% dedicated to execute on the marketing plan) then they can't implement the activity that will generate tangible value from my approach. Larger businesses have senior marketers whose job it is to build the marketing strategy and usually a matrix of stakeholders that I can't directly influence. As a result they don't always implement the work we do, which is a waste of everyone's time. There's nothing wrong with either of these types of organisations; they just aren't the right customer for my business. I work with service businesses because they have more trouble articulating what they do, and their brand is impacted by the whole business (because their people are the service they sell). In short, they have an alignment issue that benefits from *The Orchestrate Method.*

By now, you will have who you serve off-pat from the work you did in the previous chapter.

The second sentence of your value proposition needs to articulate what problem your customers want you to solve for them. In their language. Focus on the main, common problems. My customers want to scale their business and switch from being involved in everything to conducting their team to play one symphony.

What's the problem you're solving? It's important that you focus on the outcome they want, not what you do. I can't scale your business for you. But I can help you align your growth with a brand position and marketing strategy that your customers will value.

STEP 1: BENEFITS FIRST

It might help at this stage to do a quick exercise with your team. It's helpful to include one sales person and your marketer in this discussion. List three of the best features of your product or service on the left-hand side of a board or flip chart. Then brainstorm the benefits and challenge each other as to whether they're *real* benefits or not. Remember the *glass of water?* The benefit was quenching your thirst and improving your health, not that the glass holds a lot of water.

My partner and I both love music. But we listen very differently. He likes to have music on in the background when he's working at his computer. The benefit to him is it keeps him focused. I hate this. I find it a distraction. For me listening to music is an active thing - I need to be able to hear all the nuance, consequently if I listen whilst I work, I'm not focusing on the work. The benefit of the piece of music is very different for each of us.

The benefits you have listed and the information you have on the customer problems you solve from the last chapter, will give you this second sentence. Who you serve (specifically) and which problem you are promising to solve for them.

STEP 2: YOUR BUSINESS CATEGORY

The next step is to articulate who you are and what you do.

Consistency is really important when you're building a brand. One of the first things I do when I start working with a new company is ask employees one by one *when you tell someone like a friend or family member where you work, what do you say your company does?*

It's rare to get the same answer every time, yet it's important that they do - at least for that first definition. It also needs to be simple and recognisable. If you say develop the leaders of the future but actually what you mean is you run a nursery school, say so. It stops people having to get past the confusion. You think it's intrigue; they're having to compute rather than listen to why your organisation is good.

Try this with your team. Look at the answers you got. Think about what your audience defined you as. You can then complete this sentence:

<Brand name> is a <category>.

I'm a marketing consultant. I'm also a trained singer, and that intrigues people. But I lead with marketing consultant because it's *marketing consultancy* that they would search for when they need help building their brand and marketing strategy.

My friend is a therapist. He says *I'm a therapist.* He's actually a Cognitive Hypnotherapist but when he says that, people don't know what it is. Some of his colleagues use their Cognitive Hypnotherapy skills to coach business leaders. I'd suggest that they say *I'm a leadership coach*, or *performance coach.* They can then go on to explain how they use hypnotherapy to help them do that.

What I'm trying to say here is resist the urge to complicate it for people because you want them to know how much more you do, or how special you are. Your job here is to get them past the first hurdle of easily understanding what the searchable service is, so you then get the space to explain why you do it and how. Over the next week try this out with family members or new connections who aren't deep in your industry. Then pick one category and stick to it.

STEP 3: WHAT YOU DO

Next up you need to list the most important features of your service or product. Just two to three of the main ones. I build value propositions, write marketing strategies and mentor MDs and their marketers to connect marketing to the business.

Now it's your turn. Complete the following sentence with no more than three things: *We build...* or, *We deliver....* It has to start with a verb - we're looking for what you actively do.

The final and most important piece of your song is helping your audience understand *what you're not.* Rather than leaving it to them to compare you; compare yourself. Nudge them in the direction of why they should choose you. And note I said *what you're not*, not *who you're not.*

This isn't about naming a competitor. It's about comparing yourself with the main alternative route that people could take to solve their problem. For my business it's either doing it themselves or employing someone or hiring a brand agency. Knowing this means I can develop arguments for why my programmes are a better choice than any of those alternatives.

STEP 4: ALTERNATIVE SOLUTIONS

Try completing this table:

	Where clients would go if we didn't exist	Why we're better than that
1		
2		
3		
4		
5		
etc		

You will need more than one row, because there are multiple alternatives. The strongest alternative will become your core proposition but your sales people may flex to others depending on different customer motivations.

If we consider my business, a company with a big budget might hire a swanky brand agency instead of reading this book or joining our programme, but that wouldn't help their whole team connect with their new proposition. Someone with limited money might try everything themselves - but that would take a lot of time, they might not have the expertise, and they would still be playing the wrong role.

Another alternative could be hiring someone to just build their proposition. This might be a good addition to the team but it will take time and they might get caught up in the same short term struggle that the rest of the team face, unless you can give them the space and time to build it.

What are your customers' alternatives to you, and what makes you a better choice?

STEP 5: THE BIGGEST BENEFIT

Finally, you need to sum up with one primary benefit to client. What changes for the client when they use your services? Is something transformed? What do they gain? What pain do they lose?

Composers use the last few bars of a piece of music to bring closure. A piece of music usually starts and ends in the same *key* so wherever it goes in the middle it feels complete at the end; it comes back to where it started. Beethoven was the all-time master at this. His symphonies are complex and move through lots of different keys, styles and motifs. Yet he always ends by repeating the same chord over and over for a good couple of pages. He's telling you that's the end. You are left with a feeling of satisfaction - that you got to where you needed to be at the end of the musical journey.

You need to do the same with your song - your value proposition. Benefits usually fall into one of three buckets: *time, money* or *positive emotion*. Your job is to draw the link for your potential customers and show them how what you do delivers them what they want.

People will say they want a marketing consultant but they actually want a brand they're proud of, a team moving in the same direction and, therefore, a business they can grow. The benefit of working with me is I save them time in getting there without them having to spend money on a big brand agency. I also simplify what they're trying to do so it feels easier. By the end the MD has more time to focus on meeting customers and driving the business forward because they're no longer doing a bit of everyone's job and especially marketing.

Draw a Venn diagram with three circles. Write *time, money* and *emotion* in each and then see if you can fill each with how you deliver that benefit. How does what you do save the client time in the end? What does it free them up to do? How does it save them money? What does it prevent them from wasting money on? And what will feel better? What could they spend their energy on instead?

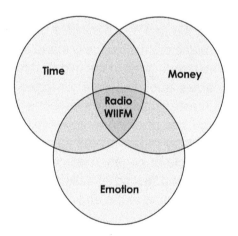

Then, at the centre of your Venn write down the *key benefit* you deliver, and check it against your customer insight. You need to tune into your customer's *Radio What's In It For Me.*

STEP 6: WRITE YOUR VALUE PROPOSITION

You now have all the components of your song, so you can write the lyrics, phrase by phrase.

- We help *<who>*

- To *<do what>*

- We are *<category>*

- We build/deliver *<2-3 key features>*

- Unlike *<most popular alternative>*

- We *<why you're better than that>*

- Which means *<what changes for your client>*

- And you *<final benefit>*

You can download a more musical version of this template at:

brandsymphonymarketing.com/tools

Whilst you build this bottom-up, starting with who you're going to serve, your audience will buy into this top down. They want to hear about the benefit first.

STEP 7: STRESS TEST

There are two ways you can stress-test your song.

1. Put it up on your wall and live with it for a while. Talk to a few people about it and ask them if it makes sense. Try talking about the benefits to a few clients. See if that's what they think you deliver for them. Do they nod (or hum along?!)

2. Get your team to stress test it for you. Ask each function to brainstorm, if this were our value proposition, what would you need to *Stop Doing/Keep Doing As Is/Start Doing/ Do Differently* for it to be most true.

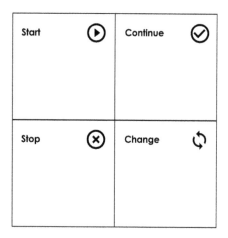

If they all say they have to stop doing your core business activity (and you weren't planning to pivot to a new business model) then your proposition isn't right. Or your business model isn't what your clients want, and you need to discuss that.

Don't be tempted to change your proposition based on every piece of individual feedback. Or shoe-horn everyone's opinion back in. Listen to it all, check it's not totally off key, and then go for it. This is your business and you need to pick the right song so you can conduct confidently.

I know it can sound like a lot of work to walk through these steps, but I can't stress how valuable it is to have this foundation. With a good value proposition; a song that the audience will love - everyone's hard work to perform it will pay dividends. The best performer playing the wrong song will at best get the review *technically gifted*. They won't get the *Bravo!* they crave.

Your *Bravo!* starts with singing the right song. Make sure it's right *before* you get everyone singing.

Chapter Eight

SCORE

A musical score makes sure that every instrument is playing their part in tune, and in time. It is also the tool by which the composer makes sure that each section or instrument is being used correctly and plays to its strengths.

A marketing strategy is, in effect, your musical score. It's not just about what you promote or advertise, but about how the whole organisation conveys your value proposition - your song - to your current and future clients.

Everything you do needs to relate back to the main melody of your song. It's used and reinforced throughout. In music involving more than one part or voice, there are three main methods of combining them.

a. **Unison** - everyone singing the same notes at the same time.

b. **Harmony** - everyone singing in time with each other but on different, complementary notes; often the melody sits in one part and the other parts enhance the sound around it.

c. **Counterpoint** - the art of combining two independent musical lines, a bit like when half your team sang *Swing Low*

Sweet Chariot and the other half sang *Oh When The Saints.* They fit together but they are significantly different.

Counterpoint is used to create momentum - the tension between the two lines weaving around each other drives the sound forward. They are essentially crafted to work together and they do periodically and eventually resolve and harmonise.

Occasionally a composer will go further and create dissonance - where the notes clash and it's hard to listen to for a sustained time. Again, this is a device that creates momentum. Organisationally speaking, this might be competition between teams - which can be useful providing it isn't at the expense of your proposition, or importantly, your customer.

It's your job to work with the marketing person or team, to define how all this happens in your organisation. Right now you probably step in to try and keep things together, or provide momentum to specific areas yourself. Nothing wrong with that from time to time but it's much better if people can do that for themselves. That they know where they're supposed to harmonise, who is supposed to lead at what point and how the handoffs work.

Imagine you go to a classical concert to hear Mozart's most famous *Horn Concerto.* Suddenly a flautist comes out on stage and plays the part of the horn instead. They play the same melody but it just doesn't sound the same. It's also not the expectation that had been created. We talked about this with Simon Sinek's *Celery Test* - don't say you're a health freak and then only be seen eating chocolate biscuits! A good (or bad!) example of this in the UK is *Three* mobile. They position themselves as busting down the norms in mobile that suck - on behalf of their customer.

When you speak to a person, they are usually very helpful. But their Voice Recognition telecoms system, which is what you encounter when you call them, is infuriating. It's one of those *Press 1 to get stuck in the system, Press 2 if you'd like us to transfer you back to the first person you spoke with* scenarios. If their proposition was low cost high automation, and the IVR worked to solve your question quickly, then fair enough. If you're positioned as the human champion, it sucks.

In her book, *What Great Brands Do,* Michelle Lee Yohn has a whole chapter about sweating the small stuff. It's important that the detail of what happens matches the promises that you make. If your employees don't realise where they fit in the whole, they can make decisions that fix their own problem but create much larger ones through the organisation. For example, a bottleneck is just moved to another team.

STEP 1: START, STOP, CHANGE, CONTINUE

We ended the last chapter with a stress-test exercise that asked people across your organisation to say what they should keep, stop, change or start doing. This was the first stage of trying to connect the dots to your value proposition. Now, make a list of the things that don't fit with your value proposition, and think hard about whether they are really necessary. I know that's easier said than done; but you're reading this because you're finding it hard to scale what you have. Maybe you have too many disparate products and that's actually the problem. Perhaps it's led to silos each of whom then brief marketing to promote their own thing, and then everyone wonders why the marketing doesn't seem clear. Maybe it's not the marketing that doesn't add up?

The critical ingredient for excellent marketing is a clear focus. You can build out from a focused success much more easily than spend time and money trying to explain the connection between disparate activities.

Tesco advertises lots of little things they do well - but they went out with their campaign about *Every little helps* before they did it. And *The little things add up* was what their customers had told them was important about shopping there. They earned permission to do it; they didn't just send lots of messages into the market.

Musically you might think of different products as different movements of your symphony. Most symphonies have three or four movements, and whilst they are all variations of the same melody, each has a very different feel. Some are slower and more lyrical. Some are faster and more furious. Sitting in the audience some people will prefer the slower movements, some the more vigorous but they link together.

STEP 2: PRODUCTS TO VALUE

It's time for another exercise. Make a list of your main products/service lines. For each, note how they solve the problem that you've focused your value proposition on. How do they make your proposition more true? Then look at their revenue potential as well as how difficult/resource intensive they are to deliver.

Are there any that don't support your proposition well, and don't deliver a lot of revenue or take too much resource to deliver? Unless they're feeder products (ie they lead onto more business as part of your customer journey) then can you retire some?

It's useful to focus your new business sales, and all your marketing support, on those that are the best fit with your proposition. You will automatically get less dissonance across your teams. Also think about where you're going; if you're pivoting, your proposition should be focused on what you want to be moving forwards, not where you've come from.

When I worked in the directory market in the noughties, we had to go through this shift. The company saw themselves as a print and online directory publisher. Consumers actually just wanted to find local trusted tradespeople and small businesses just wanted us to deliver local leads. Being a *book publisher* was the wrong value proposition. It was a means to an end for both local buyers and sellers. Like most legacy publishers their organisation design was setup to be a publisher; which made for a challenging transition.

It's also helpful here to talk about what you offer to new customers. A symphony starts out with the main theme. It's often reinforced over and over again before other variations on that theme are introduced. Think of Beethoven's *Fifth* - most people can sing *de-de-de dah*. If you were playing a snippet to market the performance that is what you'd choose and a shorter version of just the first movement might be what you'd sell to newcomers.

Think about your product set and which ones are good for new customers. What's the snippet that gets them hooked onto you enough to then go on and hear them the rest of your symphony? For a directory, this was a basic online listing for less than £100. A business could have a free one, but if they paid this small fee, they could add some text and pictures about who they were and what they did, and that increased the number of calls. It was a product that delivered value in its own right, but from which people usually upsold once they'd seen some success.

This book you're reading is a starter product in a way. You can buy this book, and just this book, and then write your own *Brand Symphony*. If you want help doing that you could then attend a workshop, or a buy a full support programme that also up-skills your marketer to play a more active role.

STEP 3: PRICING MODEL ALIGNMENT

After reviewing your products, you need to think about how your pricing model reinforces your proposition. The amount you charge is important to the revenue and profit you generate. The way you charge it - the way you package it up is actually part of positioning your brand. If you were selling tickets to a concert, would you sell one-off tickets or a subscription to multiple concerts. Are you selling just access to the concert or a broader experience, in which case is a programme, interval drinks, a CD to take home or even a drinks reception to meet the players included.

Think about the full service that you offer your customers and make sure that the added value you give - that they want - is explicitly laid out as part of the package. At *SCM World,* a learning community for supply chain leaders, events were part of that learning experience but at the point I joined they were priced separately. That actually created some dissonance through the organisation - event sales and operations saw themselves as separate from the business and no matter how much these teams were told that their job was the strengthen the overall learning, they felt and acted separate. They were priced separately and targeted as such.

At *Thomson Local* I managed a database marketing product for SMEs. Small businesses could access and export records of other businesses to mail or call on CD-ROM. We then launched an online version (this was early days of web products!). At first launch it was perceived by the sales team - and therefore customers - as the poor cousin of the CD-ROM which had won numerous awards. The shift came when we started treating it as a membership product, where customers paid for a year and got either online access, or two CD-ROMs. It was the same product via different consumption methods but there was more value online because it was always updated. We charged the same price and importantly offered the same sales commission. The positioning of the product changed in the eyes of the customer and the sales team, but it was a pricing mechanic that made that happen.

It's often the case that pricing sits outside marketing - for smaller businesses usually in finance, and as MD you have a heavy input. That doesn't need to change if you don't have a senior marketer onboard, but I would urge you to consider how your pricing model is aligned with your value proposition. Does it create dissonance for your team and customers? Does it fight with who you say you are and the value you say you deliver? (Think about the *IKEA* and *John Lewis* examples in Chapter 2).

The same goes for discounting. If you're low value and high cost, customers will be unhappy. If you're high value and keep discounting, you might not survive, because you'll get people only buying on price and erode profits.

STEP 4: PLACES YOU'RE SEEN (CHANNELS)

The next decision to make is where you will perform. Where you're seen and who you hang out with says a lot about you. A major symphony orchestra is unlikely to perform in a school hall (unless it's an educational outreach concert, where then the fact it's unusual is what makes it so special).

Think about the different positioning of *Amazon* vs. a local shop. Both offer convenience but only one is actually seen as part of the community, building and investing in it. Where do you deliver your service? Is it online? If you are a very human business, how do you signal that? A local bank like *TSB* would struggle to own their local positioning with no branches; even if their customers liked banking online, a high street presence is important. *Chanel* makeup is available in airports and department stores, but not in *Superdrug* or in smaller *Boots* stores (even when *Bobbi Brown* or *Benefit* might be). Chanel makeup is positioned as a *fashion accessory* not a *health and beauty product.*

Where you promote your services should match your positioning. This is the aspect of marketing that people most readily understand - the advertising or social media bit, or which exhibitions you attend. This is all about who you're associated with - where do you hang out and what does that say about you? Raymond Gubbay's classical spectacular concerts are often advertised in the *Metro*; a gala premiere at the *Royal Opera House Covent Garden* will choose a different media.

Here's a useful exercise for your marketer. Ask them to list out the different channels you are using and then ask them to say what the positioning of that channel is vs. yours.

For example:

Facebook	Their brand positioning	Our positioning
Finance and Leasing Association	Their brand positioning	Our positioning

Do they match? Are they using similar language and extolling similar values to you?

Look at where other brands you want to hang out with (because they're brands your potential customers buy into) are seen, even consider different industries. Where are they seen; and not? With the advent of social media this has become more important. Whilst it's interesting to think you should cover all the bases, some sites are more important to different audiences. If you're speaking to late teens get on *Instagram*. If you're talking to over 50s try *Facebook* or *LinkedIn*.

STEP 5: PROMOTIONAL MESSAGES

A key part of promoting your brand and services is your content and that is built upon key messages. Once our clients have a value proposition we also work with them to build some key messages. This is a very important part of your score as it helps you connect your value proposition with the problems it solves, and to what's happening outside your organisation. It's a good way to give your team the freedom to comment and promote you, without creating confusion or dissonance.

It's vital therefore that you undertake this exercise with your team. Ideally you'd work first with a good functional cross-section and always include the most vocal or disruptive people you have. The challenge you are giving them, as a team, is to come up with some thought-provoking messages that link to key stories in the media - and make sure they link back to your value proposition.

1st **Industry media hot topics** What they want to engage with	**Key messages** Tuning	2nd **Our services** What we want to tell them
i)	1)	i)
ii)	2)	ii)
iii)	3)	iii)
iv)		iv)
v)		v)

The first step is to review and consolidate your internal opinions. Every musical performance has a slant - two performances of Beethoven's *Ninth* can be very different if the conductor makes small tweaks but the best are those that tell a story. They emphasise something in particular that they think is most important for people to hear.

In November 2018 - the centenary of the end of World War 1 - I was part of a performance of Britten's *War Requiem*. *The Bach Choir* wasn't the only choir performing the work in that month, but our performance had readings interspersed throughout. Actors read modern war poetry and a journalist recounted her recent experience of being under enemy-fire in Afghanistan. It made for a very different performance of the Requiem which made the impact of war very tangible to a modern-day audience. It wasn't supposed to be comfortable.

Think about the articles or media you read. The people you follow are those whose opinion you either agree or disagree with. I suspect that when you set up your business you did so with an opinion about how you could do things better or differently. Maybe you want to challenge a norm or principle; *PayAsUGym* (now *Hussle*) started from the founders' annoyance that fitting fitness into his busy lifestyle was more logistically difficult than it needed to be.

Maybe you just want to do things better - *IKEA* thought you should be able to create *The Wonderful Everyday* immediately, not wait three weeks for each piece of furniture to be delivered.

I built my *Brand Symphony* programme because I felt that implementing strategic marketing and connecting strategy to activity wasn't something young marketers were trained to do, and yet in service businesses it's the key to successful growth. So, I looked for a way to engage MDs and Marketers together to build the organisation's strategic marketing capability.

Your opinion might be linked to a purpose.

Many charities actually believe they shouldn't have to exist. If no one abandoned or mistreated animals the *RSPCA* wouldn't exist. In a way, that's their opinion!

When it comes to the world of social media it's good to have a point of view. It drives debate and by default it helps you find *people like you.* However, for that point of view to cut through you need consistency - if you're pro-animals don't fox hunt - it will just confuse or even alienate people.

It's also important that the people you hire can get behind your opinion.

In 2019, as the UK was reaching the *Brexit* deadline it struck me how hard it was for the then Prime Minister, Theresa May to lead a cause she fundamentally disbelieved in. Her job was to do what the people voted for but she didn't want - a tough gig for anyone. You might deliver just what's needed but you can never over-deliver because the energy and passion you need to do that isn't there. My point is, having an opinion will also help you recruit likeminded people. Which in itself will make it easier to create a common sense of purpose behind your value proposition. Your team have to value it to push it.

So, working through your key messages, and agreeing them as a team, is vital. Once you have a list of your team's key opinions in the right hand side of the tuning fork, the next step is to research the main stories in the media that your target audience are commenting on. You'll have a sense of what to look for based on the research you did about their common challenges, but spend a bit of time searching for other relevant stories. Ask some of your clients what they read most.

List these in the left hand side of the diagram.

An example for my business would be *Account Based Marketing (ABM)*. It's been one of the hot topics in the marketing media for the last couple of years, and there's lots of media space devoted to it. I don't do ABM specifically but building a value proposition is at the core of it. If you wanted to train your marketer to do account based marketing (an individual marketing plan for every potential client) it's the same principle as doing it for your whole company. You need to make sure your proposition for each account does add up to your overall proposition or you'll just confuse people. So for me, commenting on those *posts* is relevant, but with that opinion.

When you have both sides of your *tuning fork* completed, review the cross over. Which opinions relate to which media stories? You're looking for three key messages that your organisation can credibly get behind. They should be the ones that best match both sides.

You can then give each message to someone who feels passionate enough about it to lead the charge. Using your most opinionated people will really help you here. Working against them and trying to control what they are saying is just another thing for you to chase! (If you have people who fundamentally disagree with everything you're doing though, I would question why).

If you can it's also helpful to break the messages down further to which product or service they best relate to. This allows each functional area to better link what they do day to day to your opinion and to your overall value proposition.

	Product or Dept 1	Product or Dept 2	Product or Dept x
Message 1			
Message 2			
Message x			

It's your job to review this work and make sure that everyone can link what they're going to talk about back to your clients' problems and to your song. If you're going to overrule, make sure you can explain why or you'll just disengage people; the key is using the value proposition as a guiding star. It makes the debate less about personal opinion and more about alignment.

STEP 6: PHYSICAL EVIDENCE

If you're reading this book, then more than likely you're leading a service business. If you had a tangible product that was easy to explain or demonstrate visually, it probably wouldn't be so hard for you to explain it and keep people on point. Just like a musical performance, the whole *experience* is the product people are buying from you. They take cues from the process they go through, the people they interact with and the physical evidence they see. You have to work harder to keep the emotional connection with your clients than you would if your product were always in front of them. Right now that emotional connection might be with you. But that's not scalable.

Think about what physical evidence your clients have of your value proposition. It could be your collateral. It could be emails or messages that share new insights with them. It could be you commenting on their social posts. Charities might send you a cuddly toy animal when you sponsor them, so you connect emotionally with the tiger that you clearly can't meet! A training course might give you a branded notebook, so you connect your own insights with the physical experience of taking notes.

This is why it's important to map out your customer experience end-to-end (which we will do in the next chapter). It's helpful to look at each step where you can give your customer a physical or emotional connection to something tangible.

STEP 7: PEOPLE, VALUES AND BEHAVIOURS

One of the hardest things to standardise is people. To your customers, your people are your brand. Lots of clones of you isn't yet possible and even if it were, it won't help you. Some of the most successful brands encourage their people to bring their own personality to work. Standardising the customer experience comes from allowing your people to rehearse and decide how they fit together themselves (which is what we'll look at in the next chapter). It's also important that you consider your HR recruitment and people policies as part of your marketing score.

A critical success factor is your ability to recruit based on shared values.

A simple way of defining them is to take a piece of paper and write down your own personal values on the left hand side. Then on the right hand side write down what you'd expect others to bring. Get your team to do the same exercise individually and then review what you have together.

Encourage your team to talk about what they'd expect of anyone new joining the organisation, and also get them to outline which values are so important that they think someone should be fired for not having them.

You will find some common values across the team and it's good to focus on these - only if they align to your proposition. If your proposition is about empathy yet you hire lots of efficient, process-driven people, you won't get the right result. Hiring empathetic people and asking them to just follow process will also be wasteful.

The values of the company are important and the most important factor for their success is you. If you and your leadership team don't model them, then your team won't either. If punctuality is important but you always turn up late (even for good reasons) then others won't believe you. We're back to that *Celery Test* again.

Whatever your values are, spell out the behaviours you expect to see (or not see) in order for them to be true and make those part of your reward and appraisal structure.

You get what you measure or incentivise.

SUMMARY

You now have your score; a marketing strategy that outlines how your value proposition is evidenced in the products you're focusing on, the pricing model you use, where and how people can access your service or see you talk or promote your services, the key messages you champion and the opinions you share, the ongoing physical evidence of your service, and the type of people you hire and fire.

It's now time to let your team rehearse pulling these together, note by note, phrase by phrase. To take your customer on a positive journey.

Chapter Nine

REHEARSE

Hearing lots of wrong notes in a performance isn't good. But wrong notes in a rehearsal are actually very helpful. They show you where the performance might break down. One of the key phrases I've heard when rehearsing is *sing loud and wrong.* That's because we learn from the wrong notes. Individually and collectively.

In business, people need help to define their part in the whole and then to see where it fits. Too often in organisations, the different parts only define their own roles and maybe the specific hand-off to other teams. But they never get to hear the whole piece.

In the community choir I sing with, we learn by ear. As well as the rehearsals we're given access to recordings of each individual part and also the whole. Right from the start we can hear what the audience is supposed to hear when it's joined up. In a highly-trained classical chorus the first approach to a new piece is usually an end to end sing through; sight-singing. This allows us to hear the whole piece from the start, and the conductor can hear where different parts are struggling either with their own notes, or where to find their notes from the part before.

In business we tend not to give people this chance. With products we usually test them before launching, yet with services we don't allow much time for rehearsal because it reduces active delivery of *billing* time.

This is a bigger issue when you're trying to re-position a company, or change a product or service. Getting people to learn something new is one thing. Asking them to unlearn what they already know is much more difficult. I read an article by Mark Bonchek in the *Harvard Business Review* about *organisational unlearning*. It really struck a chord. At that point in my career I was challenged with helping a directory organisation to stop seeing themselves as a book publisher. And this *unlearning* was the biggest struggle.

Rehearsals are the internal launch of your orchestrated song. It's your chance to take people through the whole score, and then let them practice. You need to give them enough of the whole to understand where they fit, as well as the focused notes for their part. This sounds time consuming but it needn't be. Investing in two or three sessions before you try a live beta version of your service, is probably all you need in an organisation of your size.

STEP 1: SING THE SONG YOURSELF

The first step is to get everyone on the same page by explaining the song. I would cover:

1. Your new proposition and why you've chosen it. It's very helpful to put this in the context of what customers have told you about the problems you solve. It positions the proposition's purpose as meeting outside needs, not internal preferences.

2. The main changes you're going to ask your team to make. Are there products that are now more or less important to focus on? Are there changes in behaviour that everyone will need to adopt? The clearer you are on what's expected the better and you should only talk about things that you personally, and your leadership team, are prepared to model.

3. That you expect collaboration to build (or rehearse) the customer journey before you're going to launch. You can talk them through the outline customer journey, by showing them the key pillars of the end to end experience you're aiming for. Talk about the types of feeling, physical evidence or products that you think are required at each stage.

After that you can get your team to validate and build on this.

STEP 2: START, STOP, CONTINUE AGAIN

Break the group into functional teams and give them 90 minutes (any longer and they will over-think it). Ask them to come back with:

a. What the value proposition means in their area (how they contribute to it).

b. How do they evidence that proposition in their function. What are the features of their service and how do they connect to the whole?

c. Any areas of concern or questions; they can list as many as they want but they can only present one back to the group (you collate the rest, it's important to digest them all).

d. List one thing they would recommend they *Stop* doing, *Start* doing, *Change* and *Continue* doing in order to better deliver on your new value proposition.

Ask each area to present back to the whole team; and then invite feedback from their peers. For example, finance might recommend they stop doing something that another area was going to build on top of. It's useful to have these discussions up front; I've never found it to be wasted time.

STEP 3: CUSTOMER JOURNEY MAP

With a smaller team of three or four people (representing different functions) you now need to work out which of the recommended changes you're going to implement and not. This is about mapping the customer journey you want and the more visual you are the better. A long strip of brown paper and *Post-it* notes can be good as it can stay on the wall and the *Post-its* can move about until you're happy with it. You can use different colours for different teams and everyone will start to see where they fit.

Always, always start with what you want the customer to experience or see across the top. It is so easy for teams to think about the process inside the organisation - the paper or data flow. What you're trying to build here is the tangible evidence of your service, for your customer. How you deliver that is secondary and probably more complicated. You might need four internal steps for the customer to experience one. We've all worked with organisations where you see (and are passed between) too many of the internal processes. I suspect they never did this outside-in exercise.

Start with just the *Continue, Change* and *Start*. Park the *Stops* for now. It's useful to see if you didn't focus on them, would they be missed? Where would the gaps be and what problems would that cause? If they're the right stops, not many.

I remember using this approach to plan a high-end executive conference - sitting with a marketing, design and event operations team. The objective was to create a joined-up customer experience. Designers needed to think about at-event signage not as *space* but as *flow* and instructions. Operations were good at considering efficient flow between rooms and efficient logistics, but less good at thinking about the order the people saw things in; the delegate usually got a massive welcome pack on arrival when all they needed at that point was how to get to the their room and check in and where to get dinner.

Marketing had been creating collateral and providing reports but little thought had been given to how and when delegates received these - rather than timing their delivery to the content of the event.

Customer journey orchestration & rehearsal plan					
Browsing	Buying	Experiencing Our Service	Contacting Us	Renewing	Leaving
On-Stage Touch Points: what they see, hear, receive, do & defining moments					
Back-Stage Processes: how they interact with each department and enabling technology					

How does this sound and what needs to change?

STEP 4: DEFINING MOMENTS

Once you have your end-to-end customer journey mapped out, think about the defining moments you want to deliver. Musically speaking, you're deciding on dynamics - which are the loudest bits; which parts have the tune when. Each department plays a more important role at different times. The key is that it looks seamless to the customer.

It can be useful to use something like this matrix to consider this point.

	Visible Customer Task 1	Visible Customer Task 2	Visible Customer Task X
Section 1			
Section 2			
Section 3			
Section 4			
Section 5			
Section X			

We've all been customers of organisations who do this badly; being transferred to the next team only to repeat yourself to another person. This would be like attending a musical performance where you only ever hear the same three-phrase tune over and over and it never develops. You're looking for the next phrase in the music, but the telephone operative starts you from the beginning again. Very frustrating. And expensive for the company.

As you build your journey look at the handoffs between parts - it's worth noting these. Ask the question - how does marketing know sales have done that? How do operations know which deliverables the customer gets when they've bought package A? How does finance know the service has been delivered and should be billed?

When you have this, think carefully about any gaps - perhaps you need new roles or to change performance targets.

One of the best skills of a composer or orchestrator is deciding which instruments are best suited to playing which part. The same melody on a flute and a trumpet sounds very different. Organisationally speaking this is primarily about functional expertise, but it's also about what the customer sees and who they interact with and when. Sometimes working with a technical person rather than a customer service person is just what the customer needs - but they probably don't sit in customer services. Any good HR professional will tell you that you also need to think about roles and functions not people. This is a big shift from very small businesses, where responsibilities are often assigned to people based on their own skills. Trouble is, when one leaves, you can never recruit someone exactly the same. Now is the time to start to think about de-marking and grouping roles together based on skills sets and you can do that based on what they do for the customer, at which point of the journey.

I worked with an organisation where the incoming leads team sat in Customer Services. The advantage of this was the team didn't get caught up in target battles so the lead could be passed to the most appropriate sales channel, based on their actual needs. After a while we realised that incoming leads needed to be serviced by slightly different people than those who dealt with issues and complaints. The latter required people who could calm the situation down; leads needed to be handled by people who can create energy and urgency to buy.

Both were providing customer service but the *instruments*

they played were different and more appropriate to different tasks. It's this kind of consideration that makes a huge difference to your brand's performance.

It's also useful to look at each part in turn and make sure there's some variety. In the community choir I sing with, the basses often end up with the percussive line. Whilst this is good for the sound, in one term every song we sang involved a variation on *dum-te-dum* for the men. It got really boring for them. So for a couple of verses the conductor switched the parts and gave them the tune. This also led to a more interesting performance for the audience. If you want high energy commitment it might be worth considering this too.

When building and launching a value proposition I always involve HR and Training. Their teams are better than me at how to reward the behaviours that reflect the proposition and values and how to dissuade those that are unhelpful. Your new value proposition might require some new training for certain sections and it's worth knowing and acknowledging that up front.

STEP 5: TARGETING SUCCESS

A critical success factor for your new proposition is targeting. If you're looking for collaboration don't target or incentivise competition. Don't let the hard work of a team reward only the most visible person.

Some parts *accompany* when others have the tune. They are equally important to the sound the audience hears, but in organisations they are often labelled *back-office*.

It's usually this back-office role that causes major issues if it's broken (remember the example of the *Ford* motor factory in Dagenham where it was the seat-stitching women going on strike that halted the entire production line?)

For each section of your customer journey list out the accompanying parts to the melody. And think about how aligned they are. Especially how aligned the goals of the leaders are. When you're thinking about targets it's helpful to think about the transitions too. Where does one team hand-off to the other and what information needs to be passed? And how do you incentivise this for both parties. A classic here is the New Business sales team handing over to a renewals team the following year. If they are also incentivised on the renewal in some small way, it will dissuade them from signing up customers who only ever stay for one year.

STEP 6: HARMONY AND COUNTERPOINT

A critical principle of singing or playing in any musical performance is that each individual has to be accountable for knowing their own part, as well as where it fits in the whole.

It's very easy to coast by standing next to a strong singer in the same part. Remember the exercise of singing *Oh When The Saints* vs. *Swing Low Sweet Chariot?* When you were walking around the room you were suddenly more exposed and accountable for your part of the performance. If you have two teams or people blaming each other, do that singing exercise with them! Coach them on how they each need to master their own part and then take responsibility for the interdependency. They have to be sure of their own part first before they can listen to the other parts. And they need to see and appreciate what happens either side of the transition in order to maintain a smooth flow across the customer journey.

Here's a good exercise to help you check how this is coming together and whether there are hand-off issues.

I call it the *Harmony and Counterpoint* check.

1. Get your customer journey map in front of you. By now you should have who is delivering each stage, and what the handover activity is - what info is passed and what the customer sees or hears.

2. Look across the full journey - are there any areas that look quite thin? Is anyone harmonising or supporting that part? Are there any sections where too many people are all doing the same thing? Musically speaking, this will sound like one part is much too loud, drowning out the others. If it's a key deliverable, or the end of the process, this might be what you want - the reinforcing chord of *we're done*. But if it's somewhere in the middle you might want to thin the sound a little.

3. Look at your *Stop* list - the things that people said they wanted to stop doing as they didn't reflect the new value proposition. Stopping some activities is a good way to signal and cause change. It also allows your team to highlight the activities that weren't adding value and replace them with better processes or products. Agree if and how they will be phased out and when, or if they have to be re-designed instead. You may have to resource their transition and I'd encourage you to do this. Of course, everyone will be keen to change others' areas but not their own so you need to task

them with looking at the whole. And remember to check if your targets will incentivise the new activities or perpetuate the old ones.

STEP 7: DRESS-REHEARSAL

A dress-rehearsal is vital. You don't launch a product without testing or a Beta, or both. You wouldn't put a bunch of inexperienced musicians on stage and expect them to just start playing. So why do it with a service?

Get a couple of people to role play being a customer and walk through the whole process - ie call in, order, get delivery - whatever the customer would do and experience.

Afterwards ask them to give feedback from their perspective. If you can use someone outside the organisation this feels more neutral and less personal if they're pointing out specific errors. Ask each team to say what they think worked from their perspective, and what didn't.

Each day for two weeks let a different person be the customer so everyone gets the full outside-in experience. Make sure your marketer is one of them.

You're now ready to perform your new *Brand Symphony.*

Chapter Ten

PERFORM

Rhythm, harmony and counterpoint are all necessary to move music (and business) forward. The dynamics and nuance you apply are what makes music work. You've now got all the notes and your team have learned and practised them. It's time for you to conduct and for your team to perform in a way that gives your customers a unique and consistent experience.

Since everyone reading this will be in a different business, at a slightly different stage, I'm going to focus this chapter on some specific areas that relate to the sales pipeline and measuring success.

One of the things that MDs often say to me is that their marketing doesn't drive sales. The MD either sits between an *it's their fault* sales and marketing fight, or they sell to their own network and their marketing is disconnected from that activity.

There are usually a couple of reasons for this. The first is that sales and marketing are mis-aligned in what they're trying to sell. Your value proposition has tackled that issue, as long as your targets are also aligned to it. The second is usually that there's no clear process or discipline around your pipeline, so hand-over and follow-up activities never get into a rhythm.

Here are some questions to ask yourself:

- How visible is your sales pipeline? Does everyone in the organisation have a way of seeing and touching it?

- Who does what? What's the journey for the customer as they move through the pipeline and who is involved at what stage? Where do marketing and sales handover?

- What is a lead? In music a lead would be a *cue*. What's the cue to handover to sales? What does the customer do or say, or what need to they demonstrate?

In a choral work like the *St Matthew Passion* I sing the 1st Alto line. There are times when the other parts are singing without us, and then we have to join them. To do that I look to the notes in the other parts to find the pitch of my first note. I work out my cue. Too often sales and marketing haven't agreed their cues in detail. So they blame each other when this handover doesn't work. No marketing automation system can handle this - the first thing they ask you when you set one up is the specific rules for the hand-off (things like how many marketing touches it's had before it goes to sales, what the demographics are of a good lead etc). I suspect one of the reasons these tools can be successful is not actually about the technology. It's that they force you to get this clear and agreed.

As a Marketing Director I've led teams who have exhibited at trade shows or events. If you ask the marketers *what did we do with the leads from last year* they often say *we added them to the database.*

This is a definitive step in the post-event process. It's clear to them what to do. After that it all gets a bit murky and involves collective people making decisions; so too often *adding to the database* is all that happens.

I've also worked in organisations where sales won't share their own prospects. They refuse to add them to the CRM system and make them visible, because they don't want anyone else to touch them. This is something that as MD you need to get involved with. That's like an orchestral musician thinking that a section of the audience will only get to hear them. Targeting and sales incentives are usually the reason behind this behaviour; the more you target for competition without a qualifier of transparency, the worse this will be.

STEP 1: SALES FUNNEL

There are many different takes on the marketing > sales funnel - just *Google* sales funnel to see a whole range. Broadly speaking I use the following stages that I'd expect a lead to go through top to bottom:

Now draw your own. What does it currently look like? What do you want it to look like? Ask your sales and marketing teams what they would expect to know about the company/individual at each of these stages and what they'd expect them to have said, done or committed to, before they can move to the next stage.

STEP 2: PROSPECT PROCESS

A helpful second step is to draw the prospect (potential new customer) process. Imagine a scenario like you've collected some contacts at a business networking or industry event. Draw the touch points you'd like the customer to go through before they buy, so that by the time they do, they know enough about you and what you can do for them, they're making an informed choice.

It's tempting here to think you'll just call them all, book a meeting and sell to them. They said they were interested, right? Wrong. If that were happening you probably wouldn't be reading this chapter. People buy from people they know and trust. You need to build a relationship with them first, that gives them some value before you ask for something from them. You need to build up credibility. This is marketing's job - to make sure that the customer can read, see and interact enough with you to trust it's worthwhile to meet.

STEP 3: CAMPAIGN PLAN

The next thing to think about is the marketing acquisition plan itself. Is there a campaign plan that fills the funnel and creates a rhythm to your marketing activities. For services marketing, particularly B2B, I'm a big fan of using events to punctuate the performance, at two to three points in the year, fairly equally spread. Your other marketing activities will lead towards each event. Expecting someone to pick up the phone having seen a social post isn't realistic. That social post might get them to view a video of you explaining how to do something; there's value in that for them, with limited commitment on their part. That video might then incentivise them to attend a webinar where they can ask questions. That webinar gives them time to consider how your service might work for their company. They might then decide to meet you at an industry event. And from that they can then feel they know and trust you enough to enter a sales discussion.

If you think about your marketing campaign through the year, events are like intervals in a performance. The audience hears the full performance but the breaks allow them to digest what they already heard before they move onto the next part. They might attend two or three different concerts by your orchestra and between each one they start to feel a greater affinity.

My first marketing role was literally for a London orchestra and the objective was to sell concert subscriptions - people committing to three or more concerts in a season and booking before the season started. This brought earlier revenue and we had a view of which concerts needed an extra push - others would go on to sell out with limited marketing spend. The most likely people to do this were those who had attended one or two individual concerts first.

Events have three features that help to embed marketing better within an organisation. They're logical lead generation points so sales like being at them; they focus teams on shorter term goals whilst still strengthening the whole proposition; and this makes aligning sales and marketing easier.

Here's a simple way of planning out your marketing calendar. If you download the Excel template from the link below you'll see months across the top, disciplines down the side. Download a template at:

brandsymphonymarketing.com/tools

1. Put two to three events in first (webinars, your own events, industry events).

2. Now list out the other media you will use down the left hand side (remember to check they're where your audience actually do hang out).

3. Then think about what could happen in those media before and after each of the events. The objectives of the social marketing or advertising might be to use content to get people to engage with the topic first and then attend an event.

Your social media, PR, advertising and emails will all be more powerful if they're linked to something like a webinar or event and they will all start to strengthen your sales activity. Musically speaking it's like a *crescendo* and *diminuendo* – getting louder towards the event then slowly getting softer afterwards.

STEP 4: ELEVATOR PITCH

Another important aspect of performance is making sure that the organisation is *on-song*. When you roll out your proposition you need to give everyone a simple elevator pitch to learn; two to three sentences that allow everyone in your company to explain what you do in the same way. It's also helpful to have five to ten slides and a PDF brochure that explain what you do for clients. Whilst sales teams may need to add in bespoke slides to cover off specific client needs, the basic elements of the pitch should be the same, and whoever is pitching will be grateful they don't have to invent the pitch every time. This also means your customers will get a consistent pitch, based on the proposition you've built. In some larger organisations I've run sales academies where sales learn to pitch the product in a safe environment, to build their (and your) confidence before speaking to clients.

STEP 5: 'ON-SONG' CHECKS

It's also useful if marketing complete quarterly checks of your key messages. If people are inventing their own ways of saying things you need to know, and then understand why. Sometimes this highlights that there's a gap in your score. Other times that people need to re-rehearse their part.

Either way you can change what you measure:

Channel or Dept	Media	Presentation	Calls	Key Areas for Improvement
Dept 1	%	%	%	
Dept 2				
Dept 3				
Dept 4				

The ultimate measure of harmony is of course whether your customers can sing your tune to someone else - ie refer you. The best measure to track this is a *Net Promoter Score,* because it's the closest to measuring behaviour rather than just sentiment.

You ask your customers just two questions:

1. How likely are you to recommend <*your company*> to a friend or colleague in your business network?

Not at all likely					Neutral		Extremely likely			
0	1	2	3	4	5	6	7	8	9	10
		Detractor					Passive		Promoter	

2. Why do you say this?

In the first question, you'll see from the above scale that 1-6 are *Detractors* (they may talk negatively about your service), 7-8 are *Neutral (*they will still use you but not recommend) and only 9-10 are *Advocates* and will create word-of-mouth.

You'd think 8/10 is enough for people to recommend you, but it's not. Whilst they will still use you, what you do hasn't been remarkable enough for them to make the extra effort to recommend you to someone else.

According to *deepinsight.com* the current average *Net Promoter Scores* for B2B are between 25 and 33, but it's quite common for you to start with a negative (ie you have more detractors than advocates) and build from that.

STEP 6: TEMPO CHECKS

It's also helpful to undertake quarterly tempo-checks through your organisation - however large or small it is.

It's important to ask all employees, every quarter, to answer an NPS and then go on to ask them if there are any areas in which the proposition is working or not working, from the point of view of executing their own role.

Also, you can ask them if there are any other areas across the business that feel off-key.

This is valuable insight but don't make it arduous. Simply send these questions out on a survey, and explain why you want the feedback. The answers will highlight where the score needs changing or maybe just that people could do with some extra *markings* from you. In music ensembles, a conductor will often ask you to add markings to a score. This might be things like *everyone breathe together at bar 9,* or *no one breathe at all in bar 2* because it's mid-sentence so please stagger where you breathe instead so that it's not audible to the audience. The score isn't wrong it's just hard to get through the whole line without a breath. The business equivalent might be the number of people who can take lunch or holiday together, or recognising that the busiest time for customer interaction is 4-5pm so team meetings can't happen at this time.

We've talked before about *Counterpoint* - creating tension by having two lines of music that fit together in places but move against each other at other points. Counterpoint creates enough tension to keep things moving and is important in organisations. It's very different however from out and out competition.

Counterpoint is how sales and marketing should work together. Sales and marketing targets should both include sales revenue and proposition consistency. Sales should be skewed more to revenue, marketing more to proposition consistency but it's critical they're both measured on the two combined.

I read an article recently that said that the Chief Marketing Officer should be the *conscience* of an organisation - they should stop the organisation straying too far from the proposition for short term revenue.

I agree with this. In a smaller business this is part of being the conductor; encouraging counterpoint but not competition.

STEP 7: AVOID SHINY NEW TOYS

Counterpoint is also relevant when it comes to innovation. When you've launched your proposition it's vital that you don't chop and change constantly. This is the hardest thing for an entrepreneur to hear, but it really undermines your credibility to immediately start talking about another shiny new toy shortly after you've launched your proposition.

You need to be out in the market spotting trends (consistent big market changes like people wanting to buy online) but not jumping on every new fad. Not every business needs an app, but I remember when everyone developed one because it was new. If something doesn't support your proposition and doesn't solve a problem your customer has and expects you to solve, then don't do it. Why? Because your team will think that's the focus now, and stop playing your symphony.

I have worked in so many organisations where employees were waiting to see what the next shiny new toy would be, before they committed to what had just been launched. Nothing really gets enough traction to become successful because nothing is given enough time to. It was a way of not being accountable for delivery.

Of course you want people to create and innovate but be careful to get them to frame the benefit of the proposal and maybe try and have a forum a couple of times a year where new ideas can be seriously discussed without distracting or derailing people from your brand performance. Ask for new ideas to be considered in light of the following questions, the answers to which should fit on just one page:

- What's the idea?

- What problem/pain point does it solve for the customer?

- What problem/pain point does it solve for us?

- How does it strengthen our value proposition?

- How will it make or save money?

- What parts of the customer journey will change specifically?

- Who or what resource will need to be involved to implement?

- What's the two-sentence headline for the press release when we've launched?

Imagine if the conductor walks off the stage half way through a performance because she's a bit bored with it after the three concerts already performed this week, and the seven rehearsals before that. For the conductor they've already done it ten times.

For the audience it's the first time they've heard it. They deserve it to sound as good, if not better, than the first time you performed it.

It's the same with your song; your value proposition. By the time it's launched you've lived it for six months. Your employees aren't yet at that point - it's still a few weeks old to them. And your customers certainly haven't heard it enough to recall it.

For a value proposition to really embed it needs at least 18 months in the market. That's driven by consistency and frequency in everything you do to reinforce it. All the things you've planned through the course of this book.

Think about all the people your *Brand Symphony* can add value to. Every single one deserves to hear your performance. So get used to conducting it.

SECTION 3

CONDUCTING THE PERFORMANCE

THE BRAND SYMPHONY

Chapter Eleven

PLAYING YOUR PART

In an orchestra, just like an organisation, there are many different roles, each equally important. There are parts that provide the rhythm, parts that take the melody, parts that harmonise and parts that provide counterpoint. Each is more or less important at different times in a symphony.

Without rhythm, it's hard for all the other parts to keep pace. A good example might be what happens to your pace when IT systems stop working? Similarly, you can't harmonise if you don't have a melody - and we've talked a lot about the impact on your marketing of having no clear song.

The conductor needs to understand every instrument and study where each part fits. But he doesn't play any of the instruments. Ever worked for a boss who constantly tells you you're not playing the right notes and then just takes over and plays it for you? I suspect you didn't work for them for long!

Imagine you're in a concert hall and the performance is about to start. The orchestra is on stage then everyone applauds as the conductor walks up to the rostrum. After about ten minutes the conductor stops conducting and walks over to the trombones. He takes the trombone off a player and starts playing his part. He then does the same to the timpanist. It would be pretty weird wouldn't it? Yet all too often as leaders we do that in our organisations. I've been there and done it. It never really helped me or my team and if any of them are reading this, I apologise. Sometimes you have to cover holidays or perhaps whilst you're trying to hire someone new to fill a role. Whilst you're playing someone else's part, the rest of the orchestra has no leader and whilst they might keep going for a while, it rarely works for long.

It's fun to think about who plays what *instrument* in your orchestra! Often you're the original composer, but sometimes it's someone else's product you're selling; perhaps a Chairman who now guides your interpretation of their work from time to time.

You probably have someone who you rely on as your first officer - whoever that is could be considered your first violin. The rest of the players look to him or her to keep themselves aligned to each other and to you. In a bigger organisation this might be a second in command such as the Finance Director, Chief Operating Officer or sometimes Marketing Director; it's they that nudge the performance into shape.

The Percussion section might be IT and/or Finance. Their job is to keep rhythm and create emphasis or pace when it's needed. The Woodwind (Flutes, Clarinets, Bassoons) often add depth to the sound, and counterpoint to create momentum; in a business this might be an operations team. Sales might fanfare your arrival like the Brass section to make sure you're heard, and the Strings are often carrying the tune and harmonising it too - delivering the service you sell and carrying most of the sound like customer services.

You might want to use this analogy with your leadership team for a bit of fun. If you're brave you might then ask them how you could better conduct and where they feel you tend to start playing their instruments for them. You're usually doing that for a reason (eg. they're not in tune or unclear) and you both need to understand why that is. Use the launch of your new proposition to re-score or fine-tune the parts.

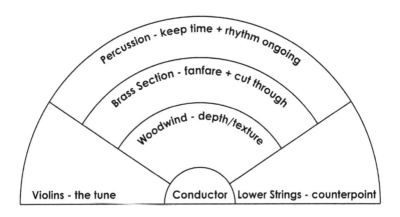

The conductor's job is to hold the performance together and make sure that it will engage the audience who have paid to hear it. You keep the players in time and tune. If one part gets a bit out of time you adjust the tempo or beat clearer to help the other parts catch up and find their way back in line quickly. If one part has a little solo that's important for everyone to hear, as conductor you create space for it to be heard by changing the dynamics (loudness/softness) of the other parts playing at the same time.

The conductor of the community choir I sing with is excellent at this. She's working with singers of very different levels and experience - some completely new to singing in choirs and sometimes the performance gets out of sync. What she does is beats more clearly to keep the other parts in line whilst she's mouthing to the part that's a bit out of time where they should be. To the audience it's hardly noticeable or maybe just for a second. But she reacts and guides quickly. If she were singing one of the parts herself she wouldn't be able to do that.

As MD of a scaling business you're no longer the composer; you're the conductor. And you need to do the same thing for your players.

It's a useful analogy, but I'm not going to tell you how to be an MD. You've built a business that's bigger than mine and I could learn more about doing that from you than the other way around. What I am going to do here is share with you what the marketer in your organisation wants from you as the MD, and what role a Marketing Director might play once you reach the right size to hire one.

Whoever develops your products and services (if it's not marketing) wants you to help them compose and create the score. They then want you to conduct. They do not want you to play their part. Ever.

The conductor's first role is to compose or choose the song that will attract the desired audience. Others have input into that but in your business it's your song and you've learned through this book that you have to pick ONE. Your marketer should be involved in that process because you expect them to get people listening to your song and ideally humming bits of it (word of mouth). It's hard to do that if they don't know it inside out and it's hard to know it inside out if you only play them the snippets you think they need to know.

In a larger organisation your marketer would lead the *Orchestration* process - build the score or marketing strategy. Your marketer is probably less experienced and you'll need to help them.

You should work with them on the customer journey that everyone will contribute to and it's at this point that you need to add your interpretation to it - the *markings* that decide where the emphasis is at any one point. At that stage it's really helpful for marketing - it's less helpful mid-performance as it breaks the momentum.

Next up they'd expect you to set targets and objectives that bring out the best of the collective performance that delivers your song.

Whilst you'll have both harmony and counterpoint throughout, it's got to be one performance. Actively targeting two parts of the organisation to compete for airspace is a recipe for dissonance.

It's audible and painful to your audience or customers and a waste of energy for your team.

I'm going to pause here.

As a product manager or as CMO, the most frustrating part of my role was always dealing with sales channel squabbles. The cause was always competition that created dissonance. In preparing to write this book I undertook a course where everyone was set individual challenges by a deadline. But if any one person didn't deliver the whole team failed. The net result was we helped each other. If someone couldn't master a particular part of the tune, we'd spend a bit of extra time helping them learn it. We didn't and couldn't do it for them but we'd help them do it themselves. There were also prizes for the best overall team (the first to get everyone over the line, for example) but there was no incentive to steal business off each other.

As you grow, please think about this.

You get what you measure and you get what you target for; and the marketer's job becomes impossible if they have to waste energy navigating that dynamic.

Your next role is to audition and re-audition the players. This means working with HR to make sure that the values and objectives you recruit, measure and performance manage to, will facilitate people playing their own part well. Give people the right instrument in the first place and you'll get a strong cohesive performance.

Of course, people want to develop and grow. You can give a bassoon player a violin and they might be able to learn it, but they will need time to do it. You have to decide whether and how you can create that time, and they also need to be willing to give up some of their own time to practise.

Finally, it's your job to lead the bigger rehearsals. This includes the first one where ideally everyone should get a sense of the whole and instructions on where each part specifically fits, before they go off and learn their own part. This is important.

With a new piece of choir music to learn, I often make my way first to *Spotify* to hear the whole a few times. Think about role playing what it is you want the final performance to sound like (or recording staged videos).

Jeff Bezos famously talks about *starting with the end in mind*, and for new services *Amazon* write the press release first so they don't lose sight of how they want customers and the market to react.

In one organisation, I remember making videos of what customers currently said about their experience and then recording actors playing the part of customers talking about a good customer experience. It visually and audibly showed the team what we were aiming for before people split into their sections to learn their own parts.

In this regard you're there to inspire and paint a picture of what you want.

You can of course attend early sectionals - sales meeting, marketing meeting, operations meeting. They are finessing and rehearsing their own parts and your role is to give early direction, then step away and let them learn it. You can then rehearse the whole and work with them on the handovers.

Finally, your marketer would expect you to welcome the audience. Meet customers, understand them, be the face of the organisation. What's super-critical here is that you stay on song.

I recently read a blog by Seth Godin about the danger of early feedback. You hear from one customer that they don't like your new proposition and you come back and say *that's not right, let's change it*. If you have spent long enough working through the steps in this book, avoid this temptation at all costs. You can't make decisions about changing what everyone does based on one person's reaction. Your job is to talk to the people who do want the value you now offer, and talk relentlessly and consistently about it. Changing the concert programme in the interval because three people left (who had to get a train, or deal with a childcare emergency, or frankly just bought a ticket to the wrong concert) would be really disconcerting. For the rest of your audience and for your team.

In short, your marketer needs you to conduct, not play. And to keep singing the same tune long enough for them to do the work that will make it cut through the noise of everyone else's song.

The challenge for your marketer is that they are less experienced than you in your business and the detail of what it really does. Without a good overall understanding it's very hard for them to tell meaningful stories about your business. If you're responsible for product development, then it's important that they understand where the roadmap is going and what the customer benefits (not features) of new products really are.

Using *The Orchestrate Method* we have broken your song into different movements.

As time goes on, this responsibility should sit within marketing and when you get big enough to hire your first Marketing Director, make that a big part of their job. I thought it might be useful to outline here what that Marketing Director should be doing.

Seth Godin wrote a blog about why product development shouldn't sit with IT. He asks *who's checking that the customer can do x?* That's because it's a marketing role. When I've worked with design teams I'm looking not at the aesthetics but whether the event delegates can read the text on the poster. A creative friend of mine, Julian Atkins, always quotes architect Louis Sullivan's motto of *form follows function.*

Earlier in my career I was product and marketing manager for a CD-ROM product. I would spend hours user-testing - working through a list of things that the customers might do in sequence, to make sure they could. Marketing's job is to provide the user stories that IT and operations develop, and then test them as if they were a customer.

It could be useful to talk to your marketer about the things they have to spend their time doing that get in the way of the most valuable activities. Sometimes they can become admin overspill - and believe that's what they're there to do. You could task your marketer to write down everything they spend their time on over a two-week period and then group them.

Ideally it should look something like this:

15% Internal comms
20% Campaign execution
20% Content creation
20% Campaign Planning & Analysis
15% Customer experience design
10% Market tracking

**Marketing
Orchestrator**

My bet is that all their time is spent creating content and in campaign execution, because they've been trying to find the story for themselves, they're asked to send out emails or posts for people, and they're told they're not delivering leads.

As you can see part of their role should be keeping an eye on market changes and news. Tracking the key stories in the media that your clients would use, sending out surveys to clients or prospects that give you insights to develop future products or share benchmarking stats. It's useful to do this twice a year.

Whilst you might come up with some potential actions or areas to investigate, it's important you don't react too quickly either. Keep everyone on track with the agreed proposition, and embedding that, until you're 100% clear another tune would be significantly better.

You can do this type of research as polls via *LinkedIn*, on webinars, at your live events or via third party media organisations or sites like *YouGov, OnePoll, Qualtrics* or even *SurveyMonkey.*

Increasingly it's seen as marketing's job to guard the customer experience. You have now worked through your customer journey in detail and your Marketing Director would be the person who needs to brief the other team leaders on what need to contribute to it. They should be attending regular sectional rehearsals to make sure that the details support the overall sound of your symphony. You will have written the song and been clear on what you want to hear; your Marketing Director should work with the other leaders to develop how it's played consistently..

Internal comms is often a function that sits between marketing and HR. Each has different skills to bring to this. If HR alone drives it, it doesn't always help the organisation focus on the customer and what's happening outside the company. Marketing can bring this context but can sometimes be poor at thinking about the engagement and behaviours required to make a value proposition live inside an organisation.

A few tips I've picked up along the way are:

- Make sure that you mix *telling* with *doing* and *listening.* Sometimes people need to hear, in your own words, what the company is doing and why.

- Try hard to think through what that means for different parts of the organisation - don't expect those people to make the link to expectations you have for each of them in your head.

- Explain the markings! Then run some practical exercises - give people ten minutes in groups to work something through and feed back. You'll quickly know if they have heard and understood.

- Have forums to listen and take questions. No agenda, *just tell me what's going on.* How can I help? Don't try to solve every issue that's raised immediately, or just bat things back. Just listen, treat each piece of feedback as an applause or boo from your internal audience. The conductor does not turn around and boo back so don't be tempted to do that. It is, however, helpful to give your perspective at the end on where you will focus your thinking on that feedback and why. Which areas you're going to look at further and any you're not and why. (It's critical to ensure you do come back at a future point; asking then doing nothing is worse than not asking.)

- Embed the key messages relentlessly. Use the value proposition to steer the conversations and the focus. Sometimes a reason you don't want to act on a piece of feedback is that it will deflect from your new song. Explain this.

- Have section leaders or voice reps. Every section in a choir or orchestra has a loudest voice. Start to think about who these people are and ideally have a mix of advocates and critics. Charge them with recommending some of the solutions to the problems themselves, including the impact on the customer and the value proposition.

- Have a reliable and regular cadence to your internal comms. It's better to meet quarterly and always have the meeting, than plan monthly only to cancel half of the sessions. You wouldn't cancel rehearsals or concerts so don't do this to your team.

- Get sales and marketing aligned and hold different forums to do this. Otherwise all the other departments get stuck between the two.

Of course a key part of marketing's role is to advertise the performance and if they have been involved in the proposition development process, it will be much easier for them to do this. They will know the story. They will know where to find case studies or stats to back up that story. They will know the relevant market issues to comment on. They will be sure that the story they are telling outside the organisation matches what the customer experiences.

When you're managing a marketer there are five questions you should be asking yourself (and them) to check if the campaigns are in tune with your song:

1. Who are they talking to? Does the copy address them?
   Never *at* them or in the *third person* (only politicians do this...
   they say things like *mistakes happened* not *I made
   a mistake.)*

2. Are they articulating the key benefits of what you do
   and the two to three most interesting features. Do not let
   them try to explain everything in detail. Consistency and
   simplicity engage.

3. Good design helps communicate things but form has
   to follow *function.* If you can't read it then it doesn't matter
   how beautiful it is, people won't get the message.

4. Is it amplifying? Does the campaign link to something
   bigger? Do you commentate on the issues that are
   important to your customers and also relevant to your value
   proposition? (Remember the *tuning fork*?)
   It's best to champion two to three key issues, causes or
   trends rather than twenty. You want to be the people that
   stand for *x*, rather than the people that stand for everything
   (again, the latter will just make you sound like a politician!).

5. Join the campaign dots together and always have a call to action for the next step. To ask someone who doesn't know you to go from reading your blog to buying your service is unrealistic. You need to take them through a journey of knowing and trusting you first.

If your current marketer aspires to be a marketing strategist and director in the future, experiencing all of this is in their development plan.

Until you have a Marketing Director it's your job to make sure that they do get that experience - they're your orchestrator in training.

Chapter Twelve

KEEPING IN TUNE

A brand performance needs constant tuning. Players will leave and new players will be auditioned and join, all of which requires a little re-orchestration or re-rehearsing. Over time additional movements (products) may also be added to your symphony.

Even without these changes, the performance can get tired and needs re-energising from time to time. Last year, I sang in a carol concert where the descant to *O Come All Ye Faithful* was different from the one I'd learned as a child. It felt natural to those in the choir who'd done this before - it was their special way of doing things that made them sound just a little different. For me it felt strange.

When someone new joins your organisation they don't just need the job description and the rules. They also need to know the norms - the *markings* that you taught everyone else a few years ago. You should also take the opportunity to ask your newcomer how it all sounds to fresh ears. Encourage them to consider their recommended changes as part of the whole performance from the start, not just change their bit. Their suggestions will be better and they will also learn where their new part fits, quicker.

Earlier on in the book we had half your team singing *Oh When the Saints* and the other half singing *Swing Low Sweet Chariot.* What if a few people now started singing *Frère Jacques* at the same time as the other two. Try it, and watch what happens! Everyone has to adjust their ears to process and hear the new overall sound. People have to work a little harder to keep their tune going whilst the new melody is absorbed. It's like that when you launch a new product - and that's when someone has made sure that the third line actually fits with the other two; which doesn't always happen. As Managing Director or CEO (or any leader) you need time to focus on things like this. Which should be possible now you aren't trying to play all the instruments yourself.

So, what does out of tune look, or sound like? And what causes it? Musically speaking it might be that the parts are not in time. They are starting and stopping in the wrong places and so the whole thing sounds like a jumble. I've seen this happen in businesses when something in one department has changed that others are unaware of. Or a new product has been launched - but customer services don't know anything about it, so they get questions about it and have to ask the customer to explain what's happening in your business.

I remember one of my first marketing mistakes; simple, and a howler. As I already mentioned, my first job was marketing concerts for a London orchestra. I proudly built a profile list, wrote a letter, created a flyer, stuffed labelled and franked all the envelopes and posted them. The other half of my job was answering the phone and selling the tickets (it was before websites and emails by the way). No one called the following day. Finally, I looked at my letter and flyer and spotted why. *No telephone number.* The lesson I learned was to check there's a clear *call to action* and also a mechanism to take it. I was definitely out of tune that day!

Another issue might be that some people are playing the wrong notes. They haven't learned their part or someone forgot to orchestrate their part. This can happen in sales led organisations where the sales person sells something that doesn't really exist and then holds customer services or operations to ransom to deliver it because *that's what my customer wants and they're willing to pay.* Selling stock you don't have isn't helpful. Listening to sales and finding out that multiple customers have an additional problem you can solve - either yourself or in partnership with others - is helpful. As long as it fits with your proposition of course.

Here are a few other reasons that your brand may keep slipping out of tune.

Your players have stopped listening to each other. In most performances and businesses this is the primary cause. People have slipped into auto-pilot or someone has siloed them. That could be a difference of opinion amongst your managers who instead of resolving the conflict, or bringing it to you, are each trying to prove they're right. It could also be that they are targeted to compete and not share or pass the baton. We've all been in these situations where we thought and even were later proved to be right so we stuck to our guns. What's often forgotten is how audible it is to the audience. For you, this becomes an extra thing to deal with. For marketing it starts to drive competing messages that confuse your audience and make your real song harder to hear.

I'm afraid to say that the second biggest reason your brand drifts out of tune is *you.* For some reason, people can't follow your beat. Maybe you're not there because you're too busy playing one of the instruments, or perhaps your arms aren't beating clearly because you're not able to give it your full attention. Are you feeling unclear on what you want - perhaps you're trying to figure something out and so your beat is too small, too tentative. If there are new ideas you're working on, try to do so with just a couple of people and keep the rest of the team focused. If you need to appoint an interim conductor then do that - but make sure they know the score and your markings.

Every so often our conductors need to take a holiday, or they have a family issue to deal with. Maybe they just need a break to plan the next performance. They always appoint another conductor to come in and lead a rehearsal and they tell that person what they want them to focus on. Someone is always there beating the time, and it's always clear to everyone who that is. Marketing is trying to follow this beat because campaigns need a rhythm to have impact. That's important. They need to be in sync, in time with the rest of the organisation. The fact that your campaigns weren't is probably a reason why you're reading this book and perhaps now you have a better appreciation of all the things that were getting in the way of that rhythm.

Another common challenge is having too many soloists. A collection of soloists is usually how a band forms, and how a company starts; a handful of really talented people who can play multiple roles and are individually creative enough to make things happen without needing a regular beat to follow. In a symphony you can have solo lines at different points in the piece; but it's usually one soloist at a time and in limited places. Lots of soloists playing their own individual tunes is one of the most unhelpful scenarios for marketing to support. Instead of being able to call on these talented people to give interviews, comment on social posts, feature in white papers or articles, your marketer ends up avoiding using them because they detract from, not strengthen, the overall proposition. Sometimes the people who helped you build your business aren't the right people to help you grow it. Sometimes they are, they just need to learn a different part in the score.

Your performance also slips out of tune when your players are unsure of where to handover. As you grow it becomes more and more important to rehearse this regularly. *The Bach Choir* has performed the *St Matthew Passion* since 1874. Yet every year there are four or five main rehearsals and anyone who has joined the choir in the last three years has to attend two additional rehearsals. It's our flagship performance so it has to be flagship.

Perhaps your issue is simply one of rehearsal; someone left and a critical task now has a workaround that isn't very stable. Or maybe the process needs re-evaluating and the customer journey map needs to change? To you this may look like incompetence, but it might not be. It's a problem for marketing if what they promise will happen when the customer calls, doesn't actually happen. Maybe leads suddenly stop being followed up; or people are under-rehearsed and your campaigns fall back out of sync with the business. Your job is to connect them back up.

Let's face facts. Sometimes the issue is that you have the wrong players. They just can't play the notes. They may need some more lessons in how to play, or how to listen to each other. They may need someone to re-write their part to be better suited to their instrument - perhaps someone left and the person covering doesn't really have the right skill-set. You can get away with that for a few bars of music, but not for a whole symphony, performed over and over. A few wrong notes in one performance is forgiven. Wrong notes in the same place in every performance isn't forgiven by the customers in your audience. You don't want to be known as the people who can't do *"X"*; for marketing that becomes a list of things to avoid talking about. Sure every performance has it's weaknesses and corresponding strengths. *IKEA* lets you take home your dream lifestyle instantly. But you might not be speaking to your partner after the exhausting process of walking around the store or building the furniture with an Allen key! Marketing won't focus on the latter. They need to know it's an issue though and they should be pressuring you to make that experience better.

Imagine you get to the end of your performance and no one applauds. The audience just leaves in silence. If this consistently happens you need to ask if your product is right for this market. If you're sure this is the market you want to serve, then your product isn't right, or they expected something different to what they got. Was it correctly advertised and performed? Or is the issue that your audience is wrong for this product. Maybe you have the best service for smaller businesses but you keep targeting corporates who need something different. Marketing often bears the brunt of this issue. They're told that the proposition is wrong, that the marketing isn't driving leads. It's worth working with them to understand why. I have definitely worked with organisations who spent too much time tweaking their proposition as it didn't sell at the first pitch. You need to have pitched it to enough people, in the right way to know this. Yes review the product but also review the score and the sales techniques too.

Don't base your decision on the fact that three people walk out of the performance. If everyone is walking out, work with the team to re-focus on what good will look like. Otherwise, keep playing for everyone who wants to hear the whole performance.

If you have no audience then yes, it's likely your marketing and sales process, pitch or people are not working and you need to address that. Honestly, the first thing I always check is if they're targeted and rewarded on the same outcome. Then check that they're focusing on the same audience and the same proposition. Finally, you can check if there's a regular rhythm to what they're doing.

Their ability to articulate this will help you understand where the problem really lies. So you can take the right action to stay in tune.

Encore

encore

/ˈɒŋkɔː/

Noun

a repeated or additional performance of an item at the end of a concert, as called for by an audience. everybody got up on stage for the final encore

synonyms: repeat performance, extra performance, additional performance, replay, repeat, repetition; curtain call the audience roared approval and demanded an encore

Exclamation

again! (as called by an audience at the end of a concert). it was Louis who shouted *'Bravo! Encore!'*

Verb

call for a repeated or additional performance of (an item) at the end of a concert. *several arias were encored*

YOUR BRAND SYMPHONY

You're now ready to write, orchestrate and perform your own *Brand Smphony.* By now you understand the importance of having a clear brand and connected marketing strategy to scale your service business.

One of the things we've focused on in this book is the importance of people playing the right parts in your performance. You might be the composer of your song, or someone else may have written the song that you and your term perform, but your role in making this happen is as the conductor. You need to orchestrate and conduct the different instruments and it's much easier to conduct if you've spent some time orchestrating. You then know enough of each part to conduct and don't have to run around the stage playing every instrument.

Once you stop playing all the parts yourself, you gain time to do more valuable things. First of all to hear and lead the whole orchestra, which allows you to keep them in tune. Secondly, you have time to welcome your audience to the performance. To greet them as they become customers, understand what's going on in their world, and have the time to consider the whole picture rather than react to individual customer stories.

The thing that most Managing Directors say to me is that they have no time because they're constantly chasing.

They also tell me that their marketing isn't working or connected to their business. I hope that by reading this book you have a better idea of how to build a marketing strategy and join the dots. To give you time to focus on the future of your business, time to think and time to hear what's really going on between the notes. Investing time in your song, your score and a few rehearsals will help you.

Orchestration is important because it enables each instrument, or each person or function in your business, to take accountability for their own part in your brand performance. That includes marketing.

In a larger organisation with a Marketing Director or Chief Marketing Officer, they would play the orchestrator role. They would break down and align your value proposition - your song - with your products, your people, your processes, your pricing model, the place you perform, how you're promoted and the physical evidence and role of your people across your customer journey. By focusing on the customer journey - or whole performance - rather than individual internal processes, you will make sure it builds towards a consistent and cohesive brand experience.

In your organisation you're probably going to play the orchestration role yourself for a while, but I would encourage you to involve your marketer as much as you can. The more they understand the whole, and the details of the customer journey, the better your marketing will be.

If right now your issue is that your marketing isn't connected there are probably two reasons; either you don't have a clear song, or you haven't orchestrated that song across the different parts. So the marketer is pushing bits out to the organisation that they don't understand, or reacting to lots of incoming and disconnected tasks. You now know the steps to take that will combat that, and it starts with the work to understand and be clear on the problems you will and won't solve for your customers.

If you need further help with your song, orchestration or rehearsals, *Brand Symphony Marketing* offers a few solutions. These include *Song Writing* workshops where we work through the elements of building a value proposition with 6-8 Managing Directors. Or *Score Reviews* where we look at your current marketing activity and highlight how *in tune* it is. We're best known for our nine-month *Brand Orchestration Programmes* where we support both you and your marketer to work through the whole five-step *Orchestrate Method.* If you'd like to see if you qualify please visit:

brand-symphony.your.scoreapp.net

You can also access some free resources for your marketer on the brand symphony portal at:

brandsymphonymarketing.com/tools

I hope you've enjoyed reading this book. Maybe outside of work it's inspired you to take up a musical instrument or join a local choir! At work I hope it helps you to finalise your composition for the next phase of your business, and get *orchestrating* the *Brand Symphony* you will conduct to great applause.

I believe that music has great power to build teams and develop relevant creativity. Music and marketing skills help ordinary people do extraordinary things, together.

I'm not special. I just found the creative intersection that comes from loving both. I look forward to hearing your *Brand Symphony* one day soon.

REFERENCES

- Bach, J. S. (1727) *St Matthew Passion, BWV 244.* Novello.

- Bantock, G (1930) *Song to the Seals.* Boosey & Hawkes.

- Beethoven, L.V. (1808) *Symphony No. 5 in C Minor, Op. 67.* Associated Music Publishers.

- Beethoven, L.V. (1824) *Symphony No. 9 is D Minor, Op. 125.* Associated Music Publisher.

- Bonchek, M. (2016) *Why the problem with learning is unlearning.* Harvard Business Review

- Britten, B (1961) *War Requiem.* Boosey and Hawkes

- Collins, J. (2001) *Good To Great.* Random House

- Godin, S. (2018) *We don't do rabbits* and *Is there a marketing person leading the IT team?* Seths.blog

- Godin, S. (2019) *The trap of early feedback.* Seths.blog

- Godin, S. (2018) *This is Marketing.* Penguin Random House

- Hosea, M. (2018) *Why marketers want to leave their job and what will make them stay.* Marketing Week, Centaur Media.

- Jobs, S. (2005) *Stanford Commencement Address.* Stanford University.

- Lavalette, M. (2018) *How to win more sales and customers*

(Jeff Bezos' 5 secrets for market penetration)
marketplaceninjas.com

- Lee-Yohn, D. (2014) *What Great Brands Do*. Jossey-Bass.

- O'Connor, J. (2014) *What is a good B2B net promoter score*
deep-insight.com

- Priestley, D. (2014) *Key Person of Influence*. ReThink Press.

- Puccini, G. (1900) *Tosca,* AMP.

- Sinek, S. (2009) *Start With Why.* Penguin.

- Sullivan, L. (1896) *The Tall Office Building Artistically
Considered.* Lippincott's Magazine.

- Notopoulos, K (2019) *Patagonia is refusing to sell its iconic
power vests to some financial firm*s. Buzzfeednews.com

- Vaughan Williams, R. (1910) *Fantasia on a Theme
by Thomas Tallis* Curwen/Faber Music.

- Ward, J (2019) *Why We Rebranded.* LinkedIn Article.

Other

- Net Promoter Score © NICE stametrix at netpromoter.com

- BrandZ ™, *Top 100 brands*, published by Kantar Millward
Brown

- Evian, *Live Young (*1998) campaign created by BETC
Agency, Paris.

- IKEA, *Wonderful Everyday* (2014) campaign created
by Mother, London.

- Tesco, *Every Little Helps* (1993) campaign created
by Lowe Howard-Spink

- Three, *When Stuff Sucks Make it Right* (2015) campaign created by Wieden & Kennedy, London.

- Willis, W. (c. 1865) *Swing Low Sweet Chariot*, Trad.

- *When The Saints Are Marching In* (c. 1896), Trad Hymn, Author uncredited

- *FrèreJacques* (c.1811), Trad, Author uncredited

- *Made In Dagenham* (2019), Dir Nigel Cole, re mention of Ford sewing machinists strike, Dagenham in 1968

- *James Bond* created by Ian Fleming in 1953, EON Productions Ltd. Musical theme by Monty Norman, key arr. by John Barry and David Arnold.

- Rick Adam, *One Man Band*: paddywhackmusic.com

- Google dictionary: definition of *overture/orchestration/ symphony/encore*

- *Rock Choir* founded in 2005 by Caroline Redman Lusher (rockchoir.com).

- *Vocality Singing* founded in 2008 by Catherine Dyson (vocalitysinging.co.uk)

- *The Bach Choir* founded in 1876 by Otto Goldschmidt (thebachchoir.org.uk)

Acknowledgements And Thank Yous

My father, Samuel Bernard Pridmore died the day that I finished the first draft of this book on 22 February 2019; which led to its dedication. But it would be remiss of me not to start by acknowledging the role that my mum, Mary Pridmore also played in my life - loving, supporting and ferrying me to all things musical and academic. And to my sister, Susan Mary thank you for balancing all the classical music and academia with a healthy dose of *T-Rex* and 70s disco!

The impetus to write this book came from Daniel Priestley and my tutors (especially Lucy McCarraher) and classmates on the *Key Person of Influence* programme. I'd especially like to thank Christine Nicholson for her encouragement, wisdom and support to keep going.

The bravery to step out of my comfort zone and take the *KPI* journey came from my partner Brooke Hender, who has had to endure every emotional reaction along the way, as well as a lot of *what do you think about….* Similarly, my own journey of personal development was supported by Beth Morgan, Anita Mitchell, Caitlin Limmer and my lifelong friends formed on the *Hoffman Process.*

The *Brand Symphony Programme* became a reality once it was visualised into a website and presentation - and I'm indebted to Julian Atkins, Jonathan Squirrell and Natasha

French at *Ocean_Barefoot & Wave Digital Experience* - for bringing it to life so beautifully.

The book became a real book, not just a manuscript, after I handed it over to Andrew Priestley and the team at *Writing Matters*. Thank you for your patience, expertise and diligence in getting my words out into the world.

I would also like to thank the early readers for your encouragement and constructive feedback - Jane Bray, Emily Foges and Anna Perkins.

Thank you to Karen Gill MBE - the inspirational co-founder and leader of *everywoman* - for writing the foreword. And Andrea Cristofaro for the illustrations throughout the book.

For the musical experiences on which I draw for this book I acknowledge Angela Moxon, my first music teacher at *Herdings Junior School Sheffield,* who made me audition for the *City of Sheffield Girls' Choir.* I would like to thank Vivien Pike and all the members of the choir from 1983 to 1994, for teaching me how to be part of an exceptional musical performance.

I also acknowledge how much I have learned from David Hill MBE and the members of *The Bach Choir.*

Similarly to Sally Duncan, Musical Director of the *Vocality Choir* Twickenham - a franchise owned by Catherine Dyson - for her sheer enthusiasm and talent in getting a cohesive performance from novice singers.

And finally to the companies who have employed me and in which I was able to hone my craft and skills – many of which I reference in this book; *Gartner, Equifax, SCM World, Thomson Directories, The Royal Horticultural Society, The Philharmonia Orchestra* and *Sheffield Theatres.*

I would also like to acknowledge Donna Robertson at Modern Muse, and the teams at *i-Realise* and *Hussle*.

I would especially like to thank the people I have directly worked for from whom I have learned so much, especially Chris Denton, Jane Bray, Laurence O'Toole, Brian Harrison, Gary Brown, Elio Schiavo, Laurence Hamilton, Oliver Sloane and Simon Puryer.

And most of all, I acknowledge all the exceptional people I've worked alongside and teams I have managed.

Too many to name individually, yet all of you have contributed to this book, by helping me learn, develop and hone the marketing techniques I use today.

Thank you all.

THE BRAND SYMPHONY

ABOUT JILL PRINGLE

Jill is an experienced Marketing Director and Consultant, and a classically-trained singer.

With over 25 years' experience leading marketing teams in large businesses such as *Gartner, Equifax* and *Thomson Local,* and as Chief Marketing Officer in a growing business, she has specialised in helping service brands clarify their value proposition and orchestrate their marketing strategy to deliver on it.

Jill led multi-disciplinary marketing teams responsible for digital product development, brand positioning, market research, pricing, sales enablement, above and below the line advertising, PR and internal communications. She has particular expertise in aligning sales and marketing activities using sales academies to roll out new products and propositions successfully. Her leadership skills earned her *Employee of the Year* awards in three different companies and her marketing teams won industry awards.

Jill has a Masters' in Marketing from Kingston University Business School and a Music Degree from Lancaster

University. Her dissertations for both were awarded university prizes for their cultural relevance.

Having sung in award-winning choirs since the age of 12, Jill learned how to plan, rehearse and execute team performances. She leverages this in her approach to building and orchestrating brand strategy. As a Marketing Strategy Consultant she now helps established service businesses (10 – 50 employees) to implement and orchestrate marketing strategies that can help them grow.

Her company *Brand Symphony Marketing* works with Managing Directors/CEOs and their leadership teams at the same time as mentoring their marketers to execute better and align marketing in their organisation.

Brand Symphony Marketing delivers *brand orchestration programme*s which combine workshops, templates and online learning to support MDs and their marketers to implement *The Orchestrate Method* outlined in this book.

Jill is passionate about the value of her musical education and its power to harmonise people and teach valuable teamwork and leadership skills. She believes that cutting music from the school curriculum is short-sighted and a disservice to the leaders of the future.

Born with hip-dysplasia (DDH), Jill also writes a blog called *diff-abled.co.uk*, to raise awareness of this common condition and she walks regularly to raise money for *Steps Charity Worldwide*.

She was born in Sheffield and now lives in South West London.

Photo credit: Nicky Adams Photography

BRAND SYMPHONY MARKETING

Marketing strategies for growing brands

Contact

- *brandsymphonymarketing.com*
- *hello@brandsymphonymarketing.com*
- *facebook.com/brandsymphony/*
- *twitter.com/BrandSymphony*
- *linkedin.com/company/brand-symphony-marketing/*

Resource Links

Download free templates:

- *brandsymphonymarketing.com/tools*

Benchmark your business:

- *brand-symphony.your.scoreapp.net/*

Lightning Source UK Ltd.
Milton Keynes UK
UKHW020634170222
398837UK00010B/419